WHAT RESPONSIBLE PARENTS NEED TO KNOW

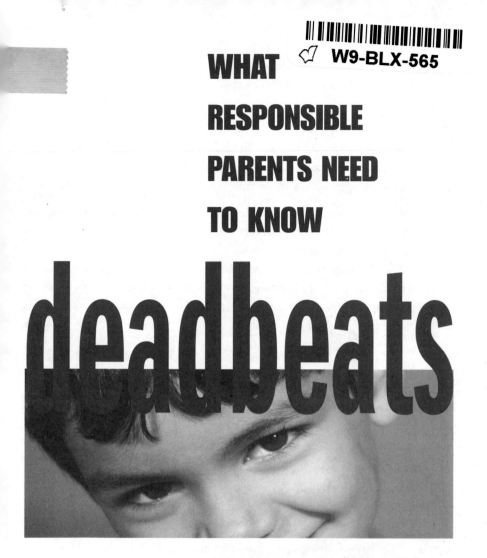

deadbeats

ABOUT COLLECTING CHILD SUPPORT

Simone Spence

SOURCEBOOKS, INC.
NAPERVILLE, ILLINOIS

This publication is designed to provide accurate and authoritative information in regard to the subject matter covered. It is sold with the understanding that the publisher is not engaged in rendering legal, accounting, or other professional service. If legal advice or other expert assistance is required, the services of a competent professional person should be sought.—*From a Declaration of Principles Jointly Adopted by a Committee of the American Bar Association and a Committee of Publishers and Associations*

Although the author and publisher have researched all sources to ensure the accuracy and completeness of the information contained in this book, we assume no responsibility for errors, inaccuracies, omissions, or any inconsistency herein. Any slights of people or organizations are unintentional. Readers are encouraged to consult an attorney for specific applications to their individual situations.

Published by Sourcebooks, Inc.
P.O. Box 4410
Naperville, IL 60567-4410
630-961-3900
Fax: 630-961-2168

Library of Congress Cataloging-in-Publication Data
Spence, Simone.
  Deadbeats : what responsible parents need to know about collecting child support / Simone Spence.
      p. cm.
  Includes index.
  ISBN 1-57071-506-8 (alk. paper)
  1. Child support—Law and legislation—United States. 2. Attachment and garnishment—United States. I. Title
KF549 .S68 2000
346.7301'72—dc21

00-024786

Printed and bound in the United States of America
VHG 10 9 8 7 6 5 4 3 2 1

important

If your children are not receiving sufficient financial support from their non-custodial parent, then you, as their primary caregiver, have the right to utilize any legal means necessary to get that parent to pay up. What you legally cannot do, and should not do, in the best interest of your children, is to deny them the opportunity to have a relationship with their other parent. Understandably, when a non-custodial parent refuses or has an inability to support his or her children, the parent who bears the responsibility may become frustrated, angry, and sometimes punitive towards the other party. Use that anger to enforce your child support order, not to keep your children away from their other parent. If the non-custodial parent is abusive in any way, or you feel that he or she is emotionally unhealthy, then take steps to protect your children during visitation. If your children are not to have a relationship with the non-custodial parent, let that parent make that decision. Please try to separate love from money. Let your children love both of their parents, but at the same time, insist that they be supported financially.

contents

items

acknowledgments

First I would like to thank my editor, Deb Werksman. She is an exceptional talent whose ability is matched only by her boundless passion for her work.

My infinite appreciation and gratitude goes to Lauren Hower, my publicist, and to the marketing, advertising, and sales departments at Sourcebooks for their intense efforts and commitment. And special thanks to my publisher, Dominique Raccah, for her vast enthusiasm and belief in this project.

A thousand thanks to my husband and my children. Without their love, this book would not have been possible.

"The duty of parents to provide for the maintenance of their children is a principle of natural law…by begetting them, therefore, they have entered into a voluntary obligation, to endeavor, as far as in them lies, that the life which they have bestowed shall be supported and preserved. And, thus, the children will have a perfect right of receiving maintenance from their parents…and if a parent runs away, and leaves his children, the church wardens and overseers of the parish shall seize his rants, goods, and chattels, and dispose of them towards their relief."

—Blackstone, 1750

introduction

The history of child support *orders* and the *enforcement* of child support has been an outrage since the day "family law" first entered the legal system. Historically, the majority of custodial families have not had *court-ordered* child support, and those receiving child support orders have rarely been awarded enough money to care for their children properly. Theoretically, child support awards should be sufficient to mimic the same economic advantages a child would have if his or her parents were together as a couple. In addition, once the court has ordered child support, most *custodial parents* still have a hard time collecting any child support monies. Some families are able to get partial payments, while other families receive no payments at all.

Fortunately, not all custodial families experience the economic abuse of child support evasion. The sad truth is, however, that only 25 percent of families that have child support awards ever collect.

This book is not written to tag men or non-custodial fathers as deadbeats, although some of them are. It is written for any custodial parent, male or female, who needs help getting financial support for his or her children. Eighty-seven percent of custodial parents are women. The remaining 13 percent are men, grandparents, and others. There are deadbeat dads, and there are deadbeat moms. In some instances both dad and mom are deadbeats. It does not matter what gender the deadbeat parent is. The object of this ball game is to get financial support for the children. That stated, for the sake of simplicity, this book will use male gender pronouns when referring to *non-custodial parents* and female gender pronouns when referring to custodial parents. Similarly, gender pronouns will be consistently applied to other roles, such as lawyers, caseworkers, and judges.

Some of the techniques in this book, when used properly, may cause embarrassment to the deadbeat. Some techniques can cause a businessperson to lose his credibility and some can cause financial ruin. That is the point. A custodial parent should feel little sympathy for someone who has to be dragged into court before he will financially support a child. Many custodial parents are ashamed that they have to force their child's other parent to pay. After all, supporting his own flesh and blood should be something that he wants to do. Others do not want to cause the other parent to become angry. It's a common misconception that a non-custodial parent will be more likely to pay child support if not forced to and if the amount of child support is low. In the eighteenth century, judges would award nominal child support awards in the belief that there would be little animosity towards a lower amount. That process of thought only causes more difficulties. Children suffer due to a lack of economic stability and often even the lower amount of money is not paid. That tactic did not work two hundred years ago and it does not work now. To award a low amount of support trivializes its necessity and meaning. Sometimes custodial parents just give up, feeling that they want to raise their child on their own, without any help from the other parent. But be assured that by getting child support you are doing the right thing for your child. Children deserve support from both parents and the problem will not go away on its own.

Part of the problem with custodial families enforcing their child support orders has been the lack of support from our government. Bureaucrats can talk themselves blue in the face over solving this issue of parental responsibility, but it has been around for centuries and not enough has been done to change it. We as a nation have not decided whether child support is a legal or moral issue. Should financial responsibility for our children be a matter that we enforce legally like other civil monetary disputes, and if so, to what degree?

There's the rub. It is a case of "free exercise of families," meaning that families have the choice of how they want to interact with each other, versus "public moral ordering," meaning that the government can decide what is best for families. Should each family decide for itself if, when, how, and how much child support should be paid, or should the government ensure that it will be done? You can see how it becomes a dilemma. Whose moral codes do we use when deciding child support? As long as child support is considered a domestic or a family issue, the nation will be split on how it is viewed.

As mentioned before, the obligation to support one's children has been around since the eighteenth century and developed in the nineteenth century under family law. Up until the nineteenth century, fathers were awarded *custody* of their children. This is largely due to the fact that since women did not work outside of the home, they were unable to financially support children. In the late nineteenth century, women began to get custody if they had some visible means of support and if the father was at fault in the divorce. At that time, industrialization and the growth of factories moved production out of the households and off the farms so as to require less help from the children of the household. Women also at that time began to take paid-labor positions, despite public disapproval.

Soon thereafter, for reasons still under debate by historical scholars, the Social Security Act of 1935 was created and included both Old Age Insurance (Social Security as we know it) and Aid to Dependent Children. Aid to Dependent Children (ADC) was created to replace a mother's pension or mother's aid program that had been created to provide assistance to "deserving widows," single mothers, and their children. In 1962, ADC was renamed *AFDC (Aid to Families with Dependent Children)*. The AFDC dole remained low until the mid-1960s. From 1965 to 1973, AFDC nearly doubled its participants and expenditures due to the rise of out-of-wedlock births, divorce, and the civil rights and welfare movements. The government took notice.

In 1974, the federal government established *Title IV-D* of the Social Security Act to set up federally mandated, state-implemented agencies to aid custodial parents in obtaining child support awards and collecting from non-custodial parents. The government's main priority in establishing Title IV-D was to the custodial parents who were on AFDC, not to custodial families on the whole, although *non-AFDC* families were allowed the same services. The program was developed to collect child support from non-custodial parents so as to lessen the financial load on the federal government. When written, it was "directed at the goal of achieving or maintaining economic self-support to prevent, reduce, or eliminate dependency." Other amendments of the Social Security Act are the Child Support Enforcement Amendments of 1984 (CSEA) and the Family Support Act of 1988 (FSA). Both were aimed at strengthening child support enforcement practices through *establishing paternity* and the collection and disbursement of child support payments. Among other things, the FSA also required that states establish and implement mandatory child support *guidelines* to produce some level of continuity with child support awards.

Seemingly, child support enforcement has had congressional support. However, the federal child support program no longer provides overall cost savings. That was its original goal, to provide cost savings to the federal government by forcing parental responsibility. The federal government supports the costs of the program, while states receive income from it. In fiscal year 1993, child support collections totaled $8.9 billion while administrative costs of the program exceeded AFDC collection by $278 million, or 3.1 percent of total collections. Because the original goal of cost savings is no longer being realized, twenty-three million children are owed in excess of $34 billion in overdue child support.

The time has come to take matters into your own hands. You cannot wait for a system that is in need of repair to collect your child support. Caseworkers are overloaded. While you can still use the services the government has to offer you, you must also be your own advocate. Remember your caseworker is there to earn a paycheck— you need to put food on your table and clothes on your child's back.

It does not matter where you are in life right now. You can be an AFDC recipient or a wealthy business owner, your child still needs and deserves financial support. If you do not need the money to raise your child, then put the funds into a college account.

Many custodial parents use their divorce attorney to handle their child support case. If you can afford one, that's good for you, but do not count solely on their expertise to get your money. Family law is not an extremely lucrative field, especially when it comes to the collection of child support. Many family law attorneys are not aware of most of the tools in this book, or more importantly, they choose not to utilize them. If you are going to use an attorney, read this book from beginning to end and the next time you have a conversation with him, ask about a few of the things you have learned. You may be surprised to find that you now know as much as, or frighteningly more than, your attorney. The knowledge you will have once you have completed this book will take you far in your pursuit of child support.

chapter 1

establishing your child support order

When Marsha and her son's father, Doug, separated, they agreed that he would pay child support to her directly instead of going through the "child support system." In her mind, it would be less of a hassle because she would always know when she was getting her money, and she thought that it would cause fewer ruffled feathers. She didn't want Doug to get angry with her for "dragging" him to court and decide not to pay anything at all. And, who wants to go to the child support agency and wait around all day anyway? She had visions of an unemployment office or a welfare office in her mind, and she did not want any part of it. She somehow felt that she was doing something wrong if she had to ask for help to get child support for her son.

Her ex made regular child support payments for about six months before the money abruptly stopped coming. For six more months he promised that the money would come, but, of course, it never did. Marsha did not know what to do and no one she asked knew either. She never thought that her ex would do anything like that. She trusted his word that he would pay child support because he promised, and she almost lost everything that she had because of it.

The moral of the story is, if you have a child and are not in a committed relationship where both parents live with and equally support the child, then you should get a *child support award* from the court. *Volunteer agreements* usually do not work. Typically, the non-custodial parent pays on a regular basis and then for whatever reason, the payments either stop or they do not come regularly anymore. Usually, the non-custodial parent is in a new relationship and his priorities and expenses have changed. There can be a variety of reasons: new car, vacation, new home, etc. Some non-custodial parents have been known to hold back child support when they are angry with the custodial parent. They use the child's support money as a means of punishment, reward, and control. Whatever the reason, it is wrong and you and your child do not need to be a part of it. For this reason, this book recommends that you immediately get a child support award from the court following the break-up of a love relationship, or when a child is born out of wedlock.

You can insist that child support be court-ordered without being angry about it. You should always be as calm, cool, and collected as you can. It may be very difficult at times, especially when you want to shout your head off or wring somebody's neck. You will always get more honey away from the bee if you do not kick the beehive. A conversation with your child's other parent might go like this:

You: Since we have decided to separate, I think that we should have a formal, court-ordered child support agreement. That way, we can both keep accurate records of payments and we will both know that whatever arrangements we have are fair. It will be less likely that we will have disagreements between us. Let's sit down and go over the expenses for (your child's name). Let's try to come to a fair agreement between us. If we cannot, then we can go before a judge and have it decided for us.

Your ex: You don't trust me?

You: It's not that I don't trust you, I just think that it will be easier this way. We both have a lot of healing to do from this break-up and I think that it will be one less thing for us to worry about.

~or~

You: I am so happy that we have a child together. Even though we are not married, I know that you love (your child's name) and me. There is something that I would like for us to do. Futures can be so uncertain, so for your protection and mine, and most importantly for (your child's name), I want to have a fair agreement between us for financial support so that we will not have any misunderstandings.

Your ex: What is this about, don't you trust me?

You: Of course I trust you! This is not about trust. I just want to make sure that we have as little to argue about as possible. As new parents we will not agree on everything, and I am sure that there will be times that we are stressed out—we do not need to argue about something as silly as money. I would rather not ask you for money when the baby needs something. If I have regular support coming in, I will be able to budget accordingly.

You will notice that in the first example the custodial parent suggested that the two parents come to some type of monetary agreement together and submit it to the court, and previously I suggested that volunteer agreements are not a good idea. I am not contradicting myself. By the end of this chapter, you will have a better idea of what your expenses are as a result of being a custodial parent. If you are offered an amount that is not fair and you are not able to renegotiate it with the non-custodial parent, you can then decide what is in your best interest—whether you should accept it or go to court. In any case, you should always get court-ordered payments. Period.

Not wanting to trust your financial future to someone who may or may not pay your child's support on time is only one reason to go through the court system. The other is to make sure that you are getting a fair deal. Your ex may offer to give you forty dollars a week to support the child. At first, you may think that it is a good offer. This book will help you determine what your child's needs are and what amount of money is necessary to meet them. Usually people forget the little things that add up to great sums of money in the end, such as weekly allowances, school lunches, and school trips. Then there are things that sometimes are not considered in the first place, but should be. For example, there may be extra medical expenses that are not covered by an insurance plan. The following list will help you to determine what you spend, or will be spending, in an average month to care for your child. Go through the list on the following pages and fill in the blanks as they apply to you.

child-related expenses checklist

Rent/Mortgage _____

House/Apt. insurance _____

Taxes _____

Water/Sewer _____

Repairs _____

Gas/Electric _____

Phone _____

Garbage _____

Food _____

Household supplies _____

Clothes _____

Laundry/Dry cleaning _____

Clothing repair _____

Car payment _____

Car insurance _____

Car repair _____

Public transportation _____

Child care _____

Baby-sitters _____

Medical insurance _____

Medical needs not covered _____

Dental visits _____

Vision visits _____

Prescriptions _____

School payments _____

Subtotal _____

child-related expenses checklist continued

School supplies	_____
School trips	_____
School lunches	_____
Dance, music lessons, etc.	_____
Extracurricular activities	_____
Barber/Beauty shop	_____
Religious affiliation	_____
Religious Schooling	_____
Books/Magazines	_____
Pets	_____
Vacation	_____
Gifts to others	_____
Allowance	_____
Subtotal	_____
Subtotal (previous page)	_____
Total Expenses	_____

Now that you have a better idea of what expenses you incur as you raise your child, you may not want to jump at the first offer of financial support you get. At the same time, it does not give you the right to pad your expenses to try to get more money either. Besides, knowing your expenses is only a starting point. You have to know what to do when you get the information.

The first thing you must do when you are ready to file for child support is to decide whether you want to handle your case yourself or if you want the state to work your case for you. Whether you handle it yourself or get the state agency to do it for you, all of the procedures remain the same. The only difference is that you retain complete control of your case if you do it yourself, but you will also have more legwork to do on your own. If the state handles your case, you end up at their mercy while they work the case on your behalf. Since they are the ones who will be filing *motions* with the court system, you will largely remain in the dark and will have to push them to advise you of any progress made. You can at any time decide to change paths if you choose a method that does not seem to work for you. If you have decided to let the state agency collect your support, you can take the case back from them at any time (provided that you are not on welfare), and vice versa. The methods that you use to enforce your child support order will remain the same regardless of who collects the money.

Which method should you choose? It's a personal choice and only you can make that decision. If you want complete control of your case and don't mind some of the headaches along the way, collect your support on your own. If you don't mind losing some control and would rather if someone else did most of the legwork for you, then let the agency work on your behalf. Most people do opt to have the state child support agencies collect their support for them. Keep in mind that it is your choice and you can change your mind at any time. If you are working with an attorney, you can still receive benefits from the state agency. Likewise, if you are handling your case on your own you can receive benefits from the agencies. Many custodial parents are routinely told they cannot have it both ways, but that is not true. Be sure to speak with someone who knows—your case-worker may not.

The first thing that you must do when you are ready to file for child support is to locate the nearest child support agency (if you are filing on your own locate the family court in your area). Every state has several child support enforcement agencies that are obligated, by law, to help you obtain a child support award and enforce your child support order once you get one. You can begin by calling your local welfare office and asking them to direct you to the closest child support agency. Although child support agencies and welfare agencies are not related, they sometimes work together. Many custodial parents end up on welfare because the non-custodial parent does not pay child support.

When you call the agency you can ask to have an application mailed to you. There is a federal law that states that, as of October 1993, applications must be provided within five days if they are mailed, or upon request if you visit the office. If time allows, pick up the application. The application should be self-explanatory. If it is not, do not hesitate to make an appointment to have someone help you complete it. You will be asked to bring in certain documentation when you go to the agency for your intake. I recommend that you get a folder, large envelope, or shoe box of some sort so that you can begin to collect the data that will help you. Although it may vary, generally the following is the information that you will need to bring on your first visit.

intake documentation

1. Birth certificates for each child
2. Your identification
3. Your Social Security Number
4. Child's Social Security Number

5. Other parent's Social Security Number

6. Last known address of other parent

7. Last known employer of other parent

8. As many current photos as you can find of the *absent parent*

If your local agency does not ask for all of this information, do your best to bring it in anyway. The more information you have about the absent parent, the better. The agency will need to contact the absent parent's employer to determine how much money he earns. It will make life much easier for everyone involved, especially you, if they already know who the employer is. If paternity has not been established at the time of your visit to the agency, you will also want to bring:

1. Records of any money the absent parent has given to you for the child

2. Records of any gifts that the absent parent has given the child

After all the information that you can supply has been provided, the absent parent will be *served* with papers requiring him to submit information on his income, occupation, current address, etc. A court date will then be arranged. Usually, a hearing officer rather than a judge hears child support cases, but it could be either. You and the absent parent will be notified of when you must appear in court, and when you do, an Order of Support will be entered. Child support that is awarded will be retroactive to the date that you filed your motion in the child support agency, and sometimes that could be a month or two. What that means is that the absent parent will owe you for several months already! For example, let us presume that you filed a motion for child support on July 1, and you finally got your day in court on August 15. If the hearing officer awarded you $75 a week in child support, the absent parent would now owe you six weeks of child support, or $450! So if you are going to file for financial support for your child, the sooner you do it, the better.

Before 1988, judges had considerable discretion when formulating child support awards. Because of that, wealthy absent parents sometimes paid very little, and poor absent parents sometimes were ordered to pay more than their monthly income. The biggest tragedy, however, was that in most instances child support awards were inadequate to meet the true cost of raising children. Thankfully, in 1988, federal *legislation* was passed (Family Support Act), which ordered all states to establish a guideline for determining child support. This helps child support awards to be more fair and realistic. Every state was ordered to adopt one of three child support formulas. The chosen formula is only a guideline, however, and if you can prove that the amount you would receive as a result is insufficient, you may be able to get a higher amount through a different formula.

income shares

The income shares formula considers the income of both parents and assumes that they will equally share the costs of raising their child together. It tries to base the support on the concept that the child should receive the same level of financial support that he would have received if the parents lived together. The income of both parents is combined. A chart listing the support amount for that level of income is checked. The support amount that each parent pays is then prorated according to his or her income. Thirty-three states, Guam, and the Virgin Islands use this formula. The following is a complete list of states that have adopted the income shares model.

Alabama	Louisiana	Oklahoma
Arizona	Maryland	Oregon
California	Maine	Pennsylvania
Colorado	Michigan	Rhode Island
Connecticut	Missouri	South Carolina
Florida	Nebraska	South Dakota
Idaho	New Jersey	Utah
Indiana	New Hampshire	Vermont
Iowa	New York	Virginia
Kansas	North Carolina	Washington
Kentucky	Ohio	West Virginia

An example based on the income shares formula is listed below:

Custodial parent's monthly earnings	$823.00
Non-custodial parent's monthly earnings	$2,650.00
Combined earnings total	$3473.00
Percentage of custodial parent's share	23.7%
Percentage of non-custodial parent's share	76.3%
Child support *obligation*	$488.00
Child care costs	$170.00
Total child support obligation	$658.00
Custodial parent's child support obligation	$155.95
Non-custodial parent's child support obligation	$ 502.05

percent of income formula

The percent of income formula uses only the non-custodial parent's income to determine a child support award. It is the easiest method to use since all that is done is a simple mathematical deduction. For example, Wisconsin deducts 17 percent of a non-custodial parent's gross income for support of one child. That figure increases slightly for each additional child. In Tennessee, however, the percentage is 18 percent and it is deducted from the non-custodial parent's net income, and, as in Wisconsin, the percentage increases slightly with each child. (Gross income is the amount of salary that a person receives before taxes are taken out, and net income is the amount that a person is left with after taxes are deducted).

The states that use the percentage of income formula are:

Alaska

Arkansas

District of Columbia (Washington, D.C.)

Georgia

Illinois

Minnesota

Mississippi

Nevada

North Dakota

Puerto Rico

Tennessee

Texas

Wisconsin

Wyoming

melson formula

Only three states have chosen to adopt the Melson formula. Unlike the other two guideline types, the Melson formula sets aside a "self-support reserve" for each parent before determining their ability to pay. What it does is allow each parent to subtract the dollar amount from their salary that is needed to keep them at poverty level before child support payments are considered. Once each parent's reserve amount is calculated and subtracted from their salary, child support can then be determined. The three states that use the Melson formula are:

Delaware

Hawaii

Montana

The guidelines work well for most people if the amount turns out to cover everything your child needs. Frequently, parents forget what they spend on their children. Use the "child-related expenses" list located at the beginning of this chapter. If you get a child support order that you feel is too low—you have forgotten too many items, or were never told to include certain items in the first place (which happens very often)—you can try to get your child support order *modified*. Chapter 4 deals with modifying child support orders.

In the meantime, other items should be included in your child support order other than child support itself. Medical insurance should be a part of your child support award. The absent parent should be required to include the child on his plan at work. If no plan is available, you can and should ask for more child support to cover the costs of a private policy.

Life insurance should also be a part of your child support award. If the non-custodial parent should die unexpectedly, your child support payments will stop. If you do not have life insurance as a part of your child support award already, you should ask for more child support to cover the costs of a life insurance policy. Naturally, your child will be listed as the beneficiary.

Child support awards are not final. They can and should be reviewed every three years. All three guideline formulas recognize that children become more expensive as they grow older, so the three-year review period allows for the custodial parent to request an increase. If you cannot wait because your support award does not include medical or life insurance, you can file a motion for a modification. An explanation of how to file a modification motion is outlined in Chapter 4.

chapter 2

establishing paternity

statistics

- One out of every four children born in the United States today is born out of wedlock.
- Only 25 percent of custodial parents who were *not married* at the time of their child(ren)'s birth obtain a child support order.
- 75 percent of custodial parents who *were married* to the non-custodial parent at the time of their child(ren)'s birth obtain child support orders.

If you were not married to your child's father at the time of her birth, you will need to establish paternity in order to receive court-ordered child support. This means that you will have to prove who the father of the baby is. When children are born between two people who are married, the law assumes that the husband of the woman who gave birth is the father of the child. When the woman is not married, she must prove who fathered her child in order to get the court system to order child support. Child support payments can always be paid voluntarily by the father, but as discussed in Chapter 1, it is not recommended in most cases.

I know a father who pays child support to his ex-girlfriend on a voluntary agreement that they have together. According to him, they do not need a formal order. Whatever their daughter needs, their daughter gets. While that sounds very knight-in-shining-armorish, I wonder if they are really splitting their child's expenses fairly. The mother has custody of the child and lives in another state. Even with court-ordered child support awards, the custodial parent usually ends up taking on more than 50 percent of the load. On the other hand, I know many fathers who bend over backward to do much more than their fair share. It's a character judgment, and only you can make the call.

The easiest way to establish paternity is during what I call "happy hour." That is when the child is first born and lying in the nursery, cute with rosy cheeks. The entire family has gathered around and friends have come from near and far to see the new baby. Of course, proud Papa is standing by grinning ear to ear at his newest creation, almost intoxicated by the miracle of it all. This is the time that most fathers would proudly announce their fatherhood.

Have him sign the birth certificate then and there. By putting his name on the certificate of birth he is admitting that he has fathered the child. In most states, that will be all you need in a court of law.

If he does not want to sign the birth certificate, or "happy hour" is long gone and you do not have an admission of paternity, you already know that you are going to have a problem. Get him to write a *letter of consent* (also called a *consent agreement*) stating that he is the father of your child. You can tell him why you want it if you do not think that he will go home and immediately pack his bags. Or, you can also make up some sentimental story about the two of you writing letters to your newborn child—whatever works.

Now, let's say that the man you believe to be the baby's father refuses to sign his name on the birth certificate or write a letter of consent. You can then have a *paternity test* ordered. A paternity test is a test that can be given to a suspected father to prove whether he has fathered a child. There are many different types of tests that can be administered. They involve testing you, your child, and the suspected father, so the baby must be born before you can begin.

The most common type of paternity test today, in most states, is a form of *DNA matching* called *Buccal swab sampling*. In this procedure, a long Q-tip type stick is rubbed along the inside of the mouth of you, the suspected father, and your child to collect cells that determine DNA. The swabs are sent to a lab, where the DNA of the suspected father is compared with that of the child in question. This test, along with other genetic procedures that can be performed, can determine fatherhood with up to 99.99 percent accuracy. Other common tests include the blood test, when blood is drawn from both parties, and umbilical cord sampling, where part of the umbilical cord of a newborn is sent in for testing.

These tests are familiar to most people. What the majority of people do not know is that paternity can be proven even if the suspected father is deceased or has not been seen in years.

Let's say that you become pregnant and you and your boyfriend are planning to be married even though his family has expressed their strong dislike for you. Before your wedding day, a terrible accident occurs and your boyfriend is killed. You were not married to him so the law cannot assume that he fathered your baby. His family doubts your boyfriend's paternity and will not help with your expenses. Meanwhile, bills are piling up and you do not have anyone to help you. To top it all off, your boyfriend was rich beyond belief. What do you do? Simple, you either have a *family calculation* study ordered (which tests the suspected father's family members for matching DNA), or you have *forensic paternity testing* or *abnormal specimen testing* performed. These are tests that can be done at the medical examiner's office before your boyfriend is buried. If he has already been buried, you can order that his body be exhumed (removed from the ground), and tested for DNA matches. Sounds gruesome, I know, but desperate times call for desperate measures. If it will keep your child out of poverty, it is well worth it.

Now let us imagine that your boyfriend is not dead, but instead says that he will die before he admits to you or anyone else that he is the father of your baby. In fact, he says he will refuse to take a paternity test so that you cannot prove his fatherhood. Do not let this type of threat keep you from establishing paternity for your child. He is trying to make you believe that if he does not take a test, you cannot prove his fatherhood, or maybe he really believes that himself. The fact of the matter is that you have the law on your side. If you file a paternity suit against the suspected father, he is legally obligated to show up for the DNA testing. If he does not show, he automatically loses, and you win. It's called *default*. You have not confirmed that he is the father, but you have won your case by default because he did not show up to defend himself and prove that he is not the father. You can then begin your pursuit for court-ordered child support. The only way the father can get out of having a *judgment* for child support entered against him is if he takes the test and the DNA does not match. This will be the only thing that will prove that he is not the baby's father. So if the suspected father threatens to refuse testing, do not let it bother you one bit. Just smile and fill out the paperwork as quickly as you can.

Now let us imagine that you do not know who the father is. You were dating two men at the same time. You slept with guy #1 for the last time three weeks before you slept with guy #2. A month later you are pregnant, and cannot be absolutely sure who the father is. In this case, both men are suspected fathers and you will have to have both of them tested. Remember, if you have only slept with these two men, one of them will be excluded completely as being the father of the baby, and the other will be proven to be the father.

If you lose your paternity case it could mean only one of two things. Either there is another man that needs to be tested, or the lab somehow went awry. You can ask to have the test repeated, but the labs rarely, if ever, make mistakes.

If you have an attorney, he will prepare the necessary paperwork to get the tests ordered so that paternity can be established for your child. If you do not have an attorney, you must contact your local *child support enforcement agency*. See Appendix B for a listing of these central offices. Call the number listed and ask them where the closest agency is to your home. Your local agency will ask you to fill out paperwork regarding the relationship between you and the suspected father, any other intimate relationships you may have had at the same time, and your pregnancy. You may also be asked to provide certain documentation, such as a birth certificate for your child, medical records, etc. A caseworker will then contact the suspected father and ask him to consent to paternity. If he does, paternity has been established and a court date for child support will be arranged. If he does not consent, then genetic testing will be ordered. Depending on your income, you may have to help pay for the tests. If you are *indigent*, you will not be asked to pay for the tests.

At this point you may be asking yourself why anyone would bother to go through all of this. That's a good question, and there are some very good answers.

Once paternity has been established, children born out of wedlock have equal benefits to those who were born within a marriage. This means that they cannot be discriminated against for any reason. If one child is entitled to two peas, then the other child is entitled to two peas. Children who are born between two people who are married, or who have had their paternity proven if the parents were not married, are entitled to many things. They are entitled to child support payments if the parents separate, medical and life insurance, Social Security benefits, veteran's benefits, if any, and rights to inheritance. You will want to establish paternity even if your boyfriend does not have a job. Just because he does not have one today, does not mean he will not have one for the rest of his life. Chapter 8 will explain how you can get child support from someone who does not have a job.

There are some women who choose not to establish paternity for their child. They are well aware of the benefits that their child will receive, but to them the drawbacks are more serious. By proving paternity in court, you are forcing a father to assume the responsibility of fatherhood—or at least the financial responsibility. The other side of the coin is that the father now has a parental right to that child. So he may then, if he has not already, file an action for *visitation*. Some mothers fear this because they do not want the father in the child's life, in some cases because they feel that the father is mentally unstable or abusive. Without legal paternity, a suspected father cannot exercise any rights to see his child.

This is a rather personal decision, and the law allows paternity to be established up until the child's eighteenth birthday. Keep in mind, however, that the child will not be entitled to child support or other benefits, and you will be on your own financially. Also keep in mind that the suspected father can take you to court at any time for paternity and visitation. You might as well beat him to the punch and allow your child the benefit of having two financially contributing parents. If you are truly concerned about the safety of your child, you can ask for supervised visitation. Be sure to have a good reason for asking for it in the first place.

Some suspected fathers will use visitation to threaten the mother of the child. They may say that if the mother takes them to court for paternity, they will take her to court for visitation of the child. Sometimes this is enough to cause a mother to reconsider her options. Keep in mind, however, that a father has a right to see his child, so he may end up taking you to court at any time. Do you really want to live with this hanging over your head? Besides, any father, or suspected father in this case, who would make that kind of threat really has no interest in his child anyway. So threats of visitation, or actual visitation, would probably go away as quickly as they came.

If the suspected father is incarcerated, is in another state, or has left the country, Chapters 7, 13, and 17 on locating the *obligor*, interstate collection, and international collection, respectively, will give you information on how to find out where he is so that you can continue your paternity case. The same rules that apply for locating deadbeats that have skipped out on their children will apply for locating suspected fathers.

chapter 3

teenagers and grandparents as parents

The majority of children born out of wedlock are born to teenage parents. When teens become parents they are confronted with special issues that others do not have.

In most instances, underage parents are not married. As discussed in Chapter 2, the law assumes that the husband of the mother is the father of her child. If she is not married, as far as the law is concerned, the baby does not have a father. Paternity will have to be established before she is able to claim who the father of her child is and get child support from the baby's father. Most pregnant teen moms live in the delusion that they will be together with their child's father forever. This prevents them from seeking court-ordered support on the basis that it might harm their relationship with the baby's father. The fathers often swear they will support and love the child forever. Here and now is replaced by promises of a wonderful future together. So, instead of filing a paternity action after the birth of their child, most teenage mothers go through the process of discovering how much it costs to raise a baby on their own. A small percentage will eventually take the father to court once it becomes evident that promises for support will not be kept. The rest carry the load on their own.

The difference between a teen unmarried mother and an adult unmarried mother is that for the most part, the adult mother has had the opportunity to finish school and hopefully get a decent job to support herself. That alone does not mean that the custodial parent in this case will survive financially. Without child support, many women end up on AFDC (Aid to Families with Dependent Children). Eighty-seven percent of the women on welfare are there because they do not get child support. An education will at least, hopefully, give the woman some type of head start. Most teenage parents do not have this benefit.

If you are a teenage parent, the information that is outlined in this book for paternity actions and child support enforcement applies to you as well. You should pursue your child support case in the same manner. Many teen parents feel that it is useless to petition for child support since the father of the child most likely does not have a job, or he has one that pays very little. Although this may be true, at some point he will become employed or his income will increase. It is best to file for support as soon as possible, because his debt begins to accrue as soon as your application is approved. When he finally does become employed he will be in arrears, which means he will owe you the money he previously couldn't pay.

For Example:

Let's say that your child's father is sixteen years old. He lives with his parents and they support him completely. He does not have a job. Your child is born and the father cannot contribute anything financially. You have one of two options:

Option # 1: You decide that it does not make sense to take him to court for money because he does not have any to give to you. Besides, you know that you cannot get any child support unless you establish paternity first and that involves testing. You have been through enough already with the pregnancy and the birth of your child and you do not want to be bothered. You decide to wait until he finishes high school, gets a real job, and makes some real money. He has promised to take care of you and your baby then. Two years later, your boyfriend graduates from high school and gets a job, but he still does not give you any money to help support your child. After a considerable amount of thought, you finally decide to take the difficult steps of filing a paternity action to establish parentage and to get child support. Months later, after you have had your day in court, your boyfriend has been ordered to pay $60 a week, and you have just received your first $60 check. You will get $60 a week, every week. That's $240 a month.

Option # 2: You take your boyfriend to court immediately for paternity and financial support of your child. Months later, after you have had your day in court, your boyfriend has been ordered to pay $60 a week. You do not get any money now because your boyfriend does not have an income. Two years later, your boyfriend graduates from high school and gets a job. You inform your case worker of where your boyfriend is working. A few weeks later you receive your first check of $340. You will get $340 a month, one hundred dollars more than your child support order states he must pay until he pays off the past-due child support.

The day you file for child support is the day that your child's father begins to owe. If it is found that he is not the father, then of course he will owe nothing. If he is the father, then the debt continues to accumulate. When he begins to make payments, he will then owe his regular child support amount, plus an additional amount to pay for the two years that he did not pay anything.

Either way, you must go two years without getting any money while your boyfriend finishes school, but the outcomes are completely different. You decide which choice makes more sense for you.

When you are underage, you are a minor by law. In most states, your parent or guardian will have to petition the court as guardian *ad litem* for child support for your child. This means that they are standing up for you in court since you have no legal voice. Your boyfriend's parent or guardian may have to stand up for him as well.

It's an interesting fact that most underage girls do not become pregnant by underage boys at all, but by adult males in their twenties, and sometimes older. An older father changes things substantially, so act accordingly.

grandparents' rights

An increasing number of grandparents have been stepping up to the plate to raise their grandchildren. Typically, these children are abandoned by their parents, who often are abusing drugs, incarcerated, or otherwise unable to care for them. If this is your case, you will not be able to get child support unless you have some type of legal guardianship over the child. Simply taking the child off his parents' hands for a while is not enough. If you want child support, you must go through the child support system.

You can get child support from both parents if the child is in your care. Once you get guardianship, your child support documents will be filed against both parents, instead of just one. You will follow the same procedures as everyone else, with the only difference being that you get double the trouble! Contact your local child support office to get started.

chapter 4

modification of your child support order

There may be a time when the amount of child support you receive does not seem as if it's enough. You may be taking money out of your pocket to cover costs that are not basic living necessities and therefore were not accounted for when you applied for child support. Items like birthday party gifts, school functions, school supplies, and trips are often forgotten when calculating child support.

If you have already been awarded child support by going to court but do not believe that the amount ordered is fair and sufficient to raise your child, you can *appeal* the court's decision. Please note that when I refer to "the court" I am referring to the person at the court who made the decision about your child support. The phrase "the court" is frequently used by attorneys and other court personnel so it's a good idea for you to become used to hearing it and reading about it. Throughout this chapter, I will either use the terms "the court" or the decision-maker. They are the ones who decide what happens with your child support. It is up to them to decide who owes, who pays, and how much. Decision-makers can differ from state to state. Filing an appeal means that you do not agree with the decision made by the court and that you want your case heard again so that another decision can possibly be made. Appeals can be tricky. You should only file for an appeal if you are certain that the amount of child support that has been ordered falls below the child support guidelines for your state or if there is a considerable amount of information that would benefit you that was not considered when the original decision was made. This is true whether you are appealing your case or if your child support award was OK when you first received it but it's been a while and you feel that it is time for your award to be increased. Either way you should be careful when you are preparing your case because of the rule of *estoppel,* which says that you cannot bring something up at a later time in order to change a decision if you knew about the information beforehand, but did not reveal it.

For example, a divorced couple agrees to an amount of child support. This agreed-upon amount is written into their divorce decree, and it is now permanent. The ex-husband later decides that he is paying too much and files papers to have the child support lowered. His reasoning is that his ex-wife's second job income was not considered when they calculated income and expenses to arrive at a child support amount comfortable for the two of them. This is where the law of estoppel is used. Since the husband knew about the second job income when the decision for child support was made, he will not be able to get his child support payment lowered.

Although I said that the couple's child support award was made permanent in their divorce decree, nothing is ever permanent in the child support world; it is only temporarily permanent. Permanent, that is, until something changes to make the current child support award not fair or sufficient anymore, and until someone makes a move to do something about it. The Federal Child Support Act of 1988 says that your local child support enforcement agency will review your child support case every three years. If a sufficient number of financial considerations have changed, your case will be reviewed and the child support amount may be increased. But, as they say, don't hold your breath. The child support agencies are so backlogged that it is difficult enough for them to handle a regular caseload. So, in order to keep up with your child support case, it's up to you to determine whether there has been a *change in circumstances* significant enough to warrant going to court.

A change in circumstances occurs when financial matters have changed considerably, rendering the original child support order unfair or insufficient. A change might result in one of two decisions: an *upward modification* of the child support order, or a *downward modification* of the child support order. An upward modification is an increase in child support and a downward modification is a decrease. Following are some incidents that can be considered a change in circumstances:

The absent parent gets a new job, or increases his income through a higher salary or a bonus.
The standards for how much of an increase in salary is sufficient to grant an upward modification varies from state to state. In many states, the rule of thumb is that the income must be increased by at

least 10 percent in order for the court to consider an increase in child support. If the absent parent receives only a 3.3 percent cost-of-living increase per year, in three years (and every three years) you will be able to petition the court for an increase in child support. If the absent parent gets a new job and is making 10 percent more than he was before, your child may be entitled to more support. Do remember that along with the absent parent's ability to pay, an increased amount of support comes only if the additional money is needed. You must prove to the court that the money you are asking for on behalf of your children is something that they need. If you are simply asking for a "cost-of-living" increase every three years, that's one thing, but if you are seeking a modification due to changed circumstances, be prepared to prove your case in court. You may want to use the income versus expenses chart on pages 37–38.

The absent parent receives an inheritance.

If you know of an inheritance that the absent parent has received or will be receiving, you may be able to seek an upward modification based on the absent parent's new ability to pay. For example, let's say that your child's doctor has recommended speech therapy, but neither you nor the absent parent has been able to afford it. Your child's speech is getting worse and you are despairing. Then, you find that your child's other parent has inherited a nice sum of money. You can then petition the court to have the absent parent pay the bill for the speech therapy since he can now afford it.

The cost of caring for your children rises as they grow up.

Children eat more, grow out of their clothes faster, and are involved in more activities as they grow older. All of this requires more money. If it is a significant amount more, your circumstances may have changed and you should petition for an upward modification.

A new medical, mental, or emotional diagnosis is made, or your child becomes ill or disabled.

If you have increased expenses due to your child becoming temporarily or permanently ill or disabled in some way, you should petition the court for more financial support from the absent parent.

These are just a few reasons that an upward modification can be granted. Use your discretion. You should always ask yourself two questions: Is the absent parent in a better paying position than he was when the child support award was granted? Is there a good reason for you to ask for more money on your child's behalf? Some changes in circumstances do not fit into any specific category so do not rule out situations that may seem unusual. For example, lottery winnings, a substantial change in either parent's tax liabilities, recommended private school for your child, etc. Also, be sure of your reasons for asking for additional child support. If you are still unsure about what a change in income is, there is more information in Chapter 8. Before you get there, however, there is a lot more that you need to know about modifications.

The saying, "Be careful of what you wish for—because you just may get it," holds true when it comes to child support modifications. You may go to court expecting to get an upward modification only to have the decision-maker look over your paperwork, decide that you are getting too much money as it is, and lower your child support award! If that happens, you will end up with a modification, just not the type you expected. You must be properly prepared when you ask for a modification. You must also have good and significant reasons for receiving the amount that your child receives now, as well as any additional monies you are requesting.

It is not uncommon for the absent parent to petition the court for a downward modification.

Some of the situations that might call for a downward modification are:

The absent parent goes on disability.

The absent parent retires.

The absent parent loses his job or has his salary greatly reduced.

There are few reasons for a judge to grant a downward modification. The main one would be that the current child support order is too high to begin with or that there has been a change of circumstances and the children do not need as much money. For example, additional child support may have been written into the agreement so that your child could have orthodontic work done on his teeth. Now that the braces are off, the additional money is not needed.

An absent parent cannot get a downward modification simply because he lost his job. While it may be difficult for him for a while, the law sees the change as a temporary condition. The child support payment must still be paid in full. A downward modification can only be made under permanently changed circumstances, in most cases. Occasionally, a judge may order a temporary modification due to changed circumstances, but it is not the norm. These situations are difficult to discuss since they can vary greatly.

Changes in circumstances for the purpose of a downward modification cannot be voluntary. They must be circumstances that are out of the absent parent's control. For example, an absent parent cannot quit his job and then claim change of circumstances and request that the child support amount be lowered. Quitting a job is a voluntary action. An absent parent cannot decide to take a lesser position where he will be making less money and request that child support be lowered. Again, taking a lesser position is a voluntary action. Absent parents cannot go back to school, sell their businesses, or take time off to "find themselves" if it means that they will request that child support be lowered. These are all voluntary actions. Absent parents cannot voluntarily reduce their income and pay less child support.

If an absent parent loses his job (which is a temporary situation and therefore not qualified for a reduction in child support), and finds another job making 25 percent less than he did at the last job, he may now be eligible for a downward modification. An involuntary 25 percent reduction in salary is substantial enough for a decrease in child support. Now let's assume that the absent parent found another job making 5 percent less than he did at the last job. He would not be eligible for a reduction in child support because most people are able to absorb a 5 percent reduction in salary.

There are other things besides child support that should be written into your child support order that may not be. If they are—congratulations, apparently you had a caseworker or attorney who actually knew what he was doing. If not, don't despair. Lucky for you, you are reading a chapter on how to change your child support order to get what your child needs.

The first item that should be included in your order is health insurance. If the absent parent has health insurance available to him through his job, the law requires that parent to cover his children. If health insurance is not available to the absent parent, but is available to the custodial parent for a fee, then an upward modification is in order for health benefits for the children.

Life insurance is another item that should be included in your child support order. If the absent parent should become ill or unexpectedly pass away, your children would be left in the lurch for financial support. Life insurance can be purchased inexpensively in any state. Have it written into your child support order that the absent parent is required to maintain life insurance in whatever amount is right for your particular circumstances. Either the absent parent can maintain the insurance, or you can have the child support order adjusted upward so that you can purchase and maintain the insurance on his behalf.

If you believe that your child(ren) will be attending college, you will want the absent parent to contribute to the financing of their education. At the very least, the absent parent should be required to foot 50 percent of the bill minus whatever contribution your child(ren) will be making themselves by working or taking out loans, etc. If your child(ren) choose an expensive school and the absent parent cannot afford it, he may not be required to pay. Take all of this into consideration.

You may be wondering if you have a child support award that needs modification. The chart below will help you to determine your change in expenses from the initial entry, or the most recent change of your child support order, to now. It is similar to the chart that you used in Chapter 1. As with any chart or checklist in this book, you may want to photocopy it so that it can be used as needed.

comparative income and expenses

	PRIOR	CURRENT	NET CHANGE
Rent/Mortgage	_____	_____	_____
Repairs	_____	_____	_____
Insurance	_____	_____	_____
Taxes	_____	_____	_____
Water/Sewer	_____	_____	_____
Electricity/Gas	_____	_____	_____
Telephone	_____	_____	_____
Garbage	_____	_____	_____
School lunches	_____	_____	_____
Meals eaten out	_____	_____	_____
Clothing	_____	_____	_____
Laundry/ Dry cleaning	_____	_____	_____
Medical insurance	_____	_____	_____
Other medical costs	_____	_____	_____
Dental/Vision	_____	_____	_____
Prescriptions	_____	_____	_____
Other drugs	_____	_____	_____
Car payment	_____	_____	_____
Car insurance	_____	_____	_____
Car repair	_____	_____	_____
Bus/Train/Cab	_____	_____	_____
Baby-sitter	_____	_____	_____
Subtotal (this page)	_____	_____	_____

Other child care	_____	_____	_____
School tuition	_____	_____	_____
School supplies	_____	_____	_____
Extra activities	_____	_____	_____
Religious affiliation	_____	_____	_____
Newspapers/ Magazines	_____	_____	_____
Books	_____	_____	_____
Barber/Beauty shop	_____	_____	_____
Union dues	_____	_____	_____
Retirement fund	_____	_____	_____
Recreation	_____	_____	_____
Vacation	_____	_____	_____
Pets	_____	_____	_____
Gifts for others	_____	_____	_____
Parties	_____	_____	_____
Birthday/ Holiday gifts	_____	_____	_____
Other	_____	_____	_____
Other	_____	_____	_____
Subtotal (this page)	_____	_____	_____
Subtotal (last page)	_____	_____	_____
TOTAL	_____	_____	_____

TOTAL NET CHANGE;
   CUSTODIAL PARENT _____
TOTAL NET CHANGE;
   NON-CUSTODIAL PARENT _____

TOTAL NET CHANGE   _____

TOTAL NET CHANGE
OF EARNINGS   _____

TOTAL NET CHANGE
OF EXPENSES   _____

TOTAL CHILD SUPPORT
CHANGE NECESSARY   _____

In order to complete this chart you may have to go through your checkbook, credit card statements, and receipts for the past year and see where you have been spending your money. Your appointment book may also contain a wealth of information. If you are anything like me, I also list events that my daughter or I have to attend, and appointments that we must keep, on my calendar. For example, birthday parties, school fair, doctor visits, etc. Make a habit of writing down everything that you do, and keep your date books and calendars for five years. They are good reference materials.

Now that you have checked your facts, you are ready to file your petition to modify your child support order. Visit the clerk of the court that handled your divorce/paternity suit or child support order and ask for a Motion and Order to Show Cause, for the purpose of a child support modification. The court clerk should have papers to give to you. If not, you can use the example in Item #1. Just be sure to follow it to the letter and have someone check it over for you for accuracy. Once the form has been completed, either you or your attorney, if you have one, must sign it and file it with (give it to) the clerk of the court. The clerk will then set a date for a *hearing*. This means that she will tell you the date on which you must appear in court. You must arrange for a copy of your motion to be served (given to) the non-custodial parent. This must be done by either a private process server or by the sheriff. There is a fee for this, generally about $15. Call your local sheriff's office and ask about their procedures. If you choose to use a private process server you can find one in the Yellow Pages of your phone book. There is usually no fee to file your motion with the court.

You will be using the same case number that you were originally assigned when you opened your child support case. That case number will follow you all the way through until your child(ren) reach legal age and are no longer receiving child support. If you move out of state, however, your case number will then change. If you have moved out of state, you must arrange for a certified copy of your divorce decree/paternity action/child support order to be filed in the court of the county where you are now living. Call the clerk's office in the new county and ask whether your copies need to be certified and "authenticated" before you send them in, or if they need to be transferred directly from the court of the previous state to the new state. Procedures can differ from state to state and from county to county so be sure to call and ask for the proper procedures in your own state and county.

Once your decree/action/order has been transferred, you will receive a new case number. You can then file your motion and have the non-custodial parent served. Be sure to serve any *public assistance* agency that you may be receiving benefits from as well. Those should be sent to the administrator. If you do not know who the administrator is, simply call and ask. There is more information on how public assistance works with child support in Chapter 10.

Item #2 is an Affidavit in Support of Motion and Order to Modify Judgment. An *affidavit* is a written statement that you are telling the truth under oath and in the presence of God, about whatever it is you have to say. In this particular case, your affidavit (your written statement—Item #2), is supporting (backing up) your motion (request) to modify (change) your support order. In other words, you have filed your request to change your child support order and get more money. Item #2 will prove to the decision-maker why the extra money is needed and that the non-custodial parent can afford to pay it. You will want the decision-maker to be aware of all your expenses before your court date so that she can be better prepared for your particular case. By submitting Item #2, you will show that you are well-prepared, well-informed, and to be taken seriously.

Since child support awards are based largely upon the income of the non-custodial parent, you will want to have up-to-date information on his income and assets to present to the decision-maker for consideration. Depending on your energy level, commitment to the modification of your child support, and your relationship with the non-custodial parent, there are a couple of different routes that you can take to determine his income and assets.

Choice #1: You can ask. Some non-custodial parents will be honest about what they have and what they earn. If the court determines that they should pay more, they will. This eliminates the need for you to take any further steps to get information.

On the other hand, some non-custodial parents will not be honest about what they have and what they earn. They may fear that the child support order will be increased and they do not want that to happen. Either they really are having trouble making ends meet and are not just "crying wolf," or they are just poor excuses for parents, or maybe both. In this case, it is up to you to decide what to do. You can go ahead and ask, or you can move on to Choice #2. However, do realize that it is not the friendliest of choices to make. If you move on to Choice #2, you are setting the scene for animosity between the two of you and maybe your children as well. These are personal choices that will affect your life, so make your decisions carefully. There are some non-custodial parents who do not deserve the consideration of Choice #1. If that is the case, I encourage you to move straight to Choice #2.

Choice #2: *Subpoena* the information that you need from the non-custodial parent or his attorney. In this case, do not waste your time asking in person for information that you most likely will not get anyway. Go for the gusto and haul out the big guns. Item #3 is a Request for Production. In this document you are asking for records of any and all monetary involvement that the absent parent has had for the past three years. This will reveal anything and everything that you need to know. It may be helpful to serve this document along with a subpoena for him to appear at a certain location so that you may ask him questions as well. Yes! It's all legal, you do not need an attorney to do it, and the non-custodial parent must appear with the documents you request or face penalties. There is more information on how to properly file a subpoena and get the non-custodial parent to show his face in Chapter 10. For now, the Request for Production can be done by mail—requesting that the non-custodial parent submit the documents you request by a certain date to a certain place. You can have them sent to your home, office, or attorney's office—wherever you choose.

When your court date comes, the non-custodial parent or his attorney will most likely object to a modification. Because you will have already done a "discovery" (a "sneak preview" look at the documents that will be shown in court—your Request for Production) there will not be too much information that he can dispute. After all, you asked for information concerning all of his money matters, and that's what you got. He cannot possibly dispute information that he gave you. The most that can be said is that your expenses are too high or that there has not been a significant enough change to warrant an upward increase in child support. This is why it is important for you to be able to prove your case.

When you have your day in court you may have an opportunity to speak. If you will be nervous, as most people are, you may want to bring this prepared speech with you. Look the decision-maker in the eye and say:

"Your honor (if the decision-maker is a judge), or Ms./Mr. ____ (his/her name should be on a name plate on the desk. If it is not, ask who will be hearing your case before the hearing begins), I have filed an affidavit with the court that I am prepared to testify to. The information in my affidavit is the information I wish the court to rely upon. If you should have any questions for me, I will be happy to answer them, otherwise, I have no further information to provide."

At this point, it is up to the decision-maker to decide whether to increase your support or not. If you have gone over the expenses versus income chart with a fine-tooth comb and it shows that you are due for an increase, then you have a good chance of getting one.

Although most of these procedures are typically done through attorneys, as I mentioned before, you do not have to have an attorney to get your modification. Just follow the simple directions that have been outlined for you and you should do just fine.

If you are considering hiring an attorney, however, the following two chapters should help you in your search. Attorneys are fine to work with if they do not charge you an arm and a leg, which most of them do, and if they really know about child support enforcement, which most family law attorneys do not. But, they do have their good points. Decide for yourself if hiring one is right for you.

MOTION AND ORDER TO SHOW CAUSE, RE: MODIFICATION

IN THE CIRCUIT COURT OF THE STATE OF [STATE NAME]
FOR THE COUNTY OF [COUNTY NAME]

In the Matter of the Child Support Order of:	)
	)
[YOUR NAME],	)
Petitioner,	)
	) MOTION AND ORDER TO
and	) SHOW CAUSE RE: MODIFICATION
	) (Ex Parte)
[OBLIGOR'S NAME],	)
Respondent	)

TO: [Obligor's Name
Obligor's Street Address
Obligor's City, State, Zip]

YOU ARE HEREBY ORDERED to file a written appearance by Affidavit in answer to the Motion and Affidavit filed by the Petitioner within thirty (30) days of the date of service of certified copies of this Motion and Order and Affidavit upon you, to SHOW CAUSE, if any there be:

1. Why the Child Support Order entered in the above-entitled Court should not be modified to increase the amount of child support to the Uniform Guidelines amount.

2. If this matter is contested, why judgment should not be entered in favor of Petitioner for Petitioner's reasonable attorney fees and court costs incurred in connection herewith pursuant to ORS 107.135.

IT IS FURTHER ORDERED that should Petitioner fail to file such a written appearance by Affidavit within the time specified herein-above, a DEFAULT ORDER shall be applied for by the moving party.

DATED this _____ day of _____, 20____

_____
CIRCUIT COURT JUDGE

IT IS SO MOVED:

_____
[Your Name
Your Street Address
Your City, State, Zip
Your Phone]

Item #1: Motion and Order to Show Cause, RE: Modification   45

AFFIDAVIT IN SUPPORT OF MOTION
AND ORDER TO MODIFY JUDGMENT

IN THE CIRCUIT COURT OF THE STATE OF [STATE NAME]
FOR THE COUNTY OF [COUNTY NAME]

In the Matter of the Marriage of:	)	
[YOUR NAME],	)	No. AS-4569
Petitioner,	)	
	)	AFFIDAVIT IN SUPPORT
and	)	OF MOTION AND ORDER
	)	TO MODIFY JUDGMENT
[OBLIGOR'S NAME]	)	
Respondent,	)	
STATE OF [STATE NAME])		
County of [County Name]	)	

I, [Your Name], being first duly sworn on oath, do hereby depose and say that:

1. I am the Petitioner in the above-entitled matter.

2. A substantial change in circumstances has occurred since the date of entry of the Child Support Order between the two parties. The change in circumstances include, but are not limited to, the following:

[THIS IS WHERE YOU WILL DETAIL THE CHANGES IN CIRCUMSTANCES. LIST ALL OF THE CHANGES AND THE AMOUNT OF MONEY FOR EACH THAT YOU WILL NEED TO COVER THEM. AT THE END OF YOUR LIST, YOU WILL TOTAL YOUR CHANGED EXPENSES AND LIST THE ADDITIONAL AMOUNT OF CHILD SUPPORT THAT YOU WILL NEED FROM THE NON-CUSTODIAL PARENT. USE AS MUCH SPACE AS YOU NEED.]

_____

[Sign your name here]

SUBSCRIBED AND SWORN to before me this _____day of _____, 20___.

_____

NOTARY PUBLIC FOR [YOUR STATE NAME]   My Commission expires: _____

REQUEST FOR PRODUCTION
IN THE CIRCUIT COURT OF THE STATE OF [STATE NAME]
FOR THE COUNTY OF [COUNTY NAME]

In the Matter of the Marriage of:)

)

[YOUR NAME],   )

    Petitioner,   )

)   REQUEST FOR PRODUCTION

    and   )

)

[OBLIGOR'S NAME],   )

    Respondent,   )

TO: [Obligor's Name], Respondent

Pursuant to ORCP 43, Petitioner hereby requests that Respondent produce and permit the party making this request to inspect and copy all documents described in this request by _____, on the ___ day of _____, 20____.

As used in this request, the term "Documents" means and includes, without limitation, the following whether printed or recorded or reproduced by hand, and draft, duplicates, carbon copies, or any other copies thereof: agreements, communications, correspondence, telegrams, memoranda, summaries or records of telephone conversations, summaries or records of personal conversations or interviews, diaries, graphs, reports, notebooks, statements, plans, drawings, sketches, maps, photographs, contracts, licenses, ledgers, books of account, vouchers, bank checks, charge slips, credit memoranda, receipts, audit papers, working papers, statistical records, cost sheets, loan files, drafts, letters, any marginal comments appearing on any documents, and all other writings or papers similar to any of the foregoing, including information maintained on computer media.

Documents requested are all those in your possession, or in the possession of your attorney, or under your control or available to you, specifically the following:

1. All federal and state income tax returns for the tax years _____ through _____, inclusive, and documents showing any estimated taxes paid for tax years for which tax returns have not yet been filed, for you, together with copies of all partnership information returns prepared by or on behalf of any partnership to which you belonged during the same period.
2. All federal and state income tax returns for the tax years _____ through _____, inclusive, filed by any closely held corporation, limited partnership, or other entity in which you have, or had, an interest.
3. Any list of personal property prepared by either party.
4. All documents reflecting your income from all sources from _____ to date, including, but not limited to, W-2s, 1099s, wage statements, and paycheck stubs.
5. All documents showing any interest you have in real or personal property, including deeds, contracts, vehicle registration, titles, bills of sale, and any other documents concerning any assets in which you have claim or may claim any interest.
6. All documents showing any existence and nature of any security interest in any asset owned by you or any asset in which you claim an interest, including, but not limited to, mortgages, trust deeds, and security agreements.

Item #3: Request for Production

7. All documents relating to the purchase of any real or personal property in which you have an interest, together along with any closing statements prepared in connection with the purchase by you of any interest in real property.
8. All tax statements on any real property, business interest, or personal property owned by either party.
9. All financial statements prepared by or for you during the preceding five (5) years and loan applications submitted by you or any entity in which you have an interest to any bank or other lending institution or insurance company in connection with any application for a loan from _____ to date.
10. All documents evidencing your ownership or interest in any general partnership, limited partnership, or closely held corporation in which you owned an interest at any time from _____ to the present, or in which you now own an interest, including any buy and sell agreements, stock purchase agreements, and partnership agreements.
11. All documents which reflect the amount, location, and value of any stocks or bonds owned either jointly or individually by you.
12. All documents which reflect the amount and location of any checking accounts, savings accounts, money markets, stock brokerage, or other financial institution accounts or similar accounts on which your name appears, or has appeared, on which you are or were a signer, or on which you have had funds or securities on deposit, including periodic statements, canceled checks, check registers (and/or stubs), deposit records, passbooks, and certificates of deposit for the period _____ to date.
13. Records of all charge accounts, credit accounts, and lines of credit, including copies of all statements reflecting charges made and payments received on said accounts from the period _____ to date.
14. All policies of insurance on the life of either party, together with all records related thereto.
15. All receipts reflecting cash purchases to you from _____ to date.
16. List of all safe deposit boxes to which you have access, and a list of all the contents of any such safe deposit boxes.
17. All records of all trusts, estates, life estates, or other property in which you have any beneficial interest whatsoever, including a remainder interest or contingent remainder interest.
18. All appraisals prepared by anyone for any real property in which either party has any interest.
19. Any and all stock options or stock benefits between you and your employer, and any information concerning receipt of such stock for the past five (5) years.
20. All documents concerning any pension, profit sharing, retirement, vacation, savings, PERS, IRA, SEP, KEOGH, 401k, Social Security, veteran's benefits, deferred compensation, or other similar plans, programs, or accounts (past or present), including any and all statements reflecting your interest therein, any summary description of the plan, a copy of the plan, the name and address of the trustee, custodial and/or plan administrator, or other officer in charge of each account or plan.
21. All records reflecting all income received by _____(husband, wife, girlfriend, boyfriend) from all sources, from _____ to date.
22. All records relating to any expenses or sums paid by you for which you have received reimbursement from your private practice, or your _____ association/employment with _____.
23. All records of all trusts, estates, life estates, or any other property in which you have any beneficial interest whatsoever, including a remainder interest or a contingent remainder interest, including, but not limited to, any Last Will and Testament, Codicil, or other instrument or bequest which names you as a beneficiary or contingent beneficiary.
24. Your current last Will and Testament, together with any Codicils related thereto.
25. All stock certificates, bonds, indentures, or any other security in which you claim an interest of any kind.

Item #3: Request for Production continued

26. All health, medical, accident, hospital, and dental insurance policies covering you or any member of your family.
27. All records reflecting any indebtedness that you owe, including, but not limited to, notes and contracts.
28. Any records reflecting any guarantee made by either party.
29. All documents or correspondence concerning any credit extended by you or any debt owed to you by anyone.
30. All documents concerning any benefits available to you under any programs, Social Security, veteran's benefits, or any other program, private or public, under which you may have a claim for future payments of any kind or nature.
31. All documents listing, describing, or showing the existence of personal property, jewelry, gold, silver, precious metals, gems, artwork, antiques, coins, stamp collections, or other similar assets in which you claim an interest.
32. Copies of all documents showing the existence of any lawsuit or claim against you or your spouse or by you or your spouse against any person or entity.
33. All documents showing any gifts, transfers, or sales made by you of any asset with a value in excess of $500 during the preceding thirty-six (36) months.
34. All documents showing the existence or describing any furniture, fixtures, office equipment, or other similar assets owned by you.
35. All documents showing any farm implements, farm or logging equipment, tools, or other equipment or machinery owned by you or in which you claim an interest.
36. All records showing any interest held by you in any livestock, horses, or any animal and all documentation showing the value thereof.
37. All documents showing any interest you have in any patent, trademark, copyright, royalty, or other intangible asset.
38. All powers of attorney executed by you during the preceding three (3) years.
39. All documents of any kind or nature showing the existence or value of any asset of any kind or nature in which you claim any interest whatsoever.

****

This request is a continuing request. If the documents requested above come into the possession or control of you or your attorneys after the date requested for the production herein, Petitioner requests that they be produced at the time of their availability.

DATED this _____ day of _____, 20___.

_____
[Your Name
Your Street Address
Your City, Your State, Your Zip Code
Your Phone]

chapter 5

finding and hiring an attorney

The first thing that most people consider when they are trying to collect child support is hiring an attorney. Having an attorney can make your life a lot easier since he can negotiate the legal system on your behalf. On the other hand, an attorney can also make your life a living hell if he does not know how to handle child support enforcement cases correctly. You can pay an attorney to work for you if you can afford it, you can find an attorney to work for you for free if you are indigent, or you can pursue your child support case *pro se* (without an attorney). This chapter will deal with hiring an attorney whom you must pay, and how to creatively pay an attorney's fee.

If you are considering hiring a lawyer, there are some things that you should know first.

Fact #1: You are the boss. Your lawyer may know how to work the legal system, he may have taken a course in Intimidation 101, and he may be able to muddle through the paperwork more easily than you can. The key word, however, is, "hire." You are hiring the lawyer, you are paying the lawyer. You are the boss. Your boss may have hired you for your expertise in the job that you do, but she is your boss. She sees to it that you are paid. If she is not happy with the job that you are doing she is sure to let you know. Your boss may even fire you, if necessary. You need to take the same attitude with the lawyer you hire. You are the boss. If you do not like the services that you are receiving, be sure to let your "employee" know. If worse comes to worst, you can fire your lawyer and get another one. We will get back to that later.

Fact #2: Your "expert" may not be an expert at all. Just because someone has attended law school does not mean that he is a good lawyer; it also does not mean that he can effectively practice any particular type of law. If you were a pregnant woman, whom would you go to—an obstetrician or a cardiologist? If you had a choice, you would probably go to the obstetrician, because they are the ones who have been trained in medical school to help deliver healthy babies. A cardiologist could probably deliver a baby too, if necessary—most doctors could. An obstetrician, however, has been specifically trained to help pregnant women.

It's the same with lawyers. Most lawyers could practice any kind of law if they had to. All they would have to do is spend a few days in the law library doing some research and most people would never know the difference. The majority of lawyers, however, do have some kind of specialty. There are real estate lawyers, criminal lawyers, malpractice lawyers, etc. Of course, you will want a lawyer who practices family law. For this reason, it is not advisable to work with your cousin the real estate attorney, or your best friend's father, the criminal attorney, even though you know they have your best interests at heart. Law is a learned trade. The criminal attorney has spent his time learning criminal law, and the real estate attorney has spent his time learning real estate law. Family law attorneys have spent their time learning family law (under which child support falls), but they may not know how to get it collected once it's due. Remember, just because a lawyer is a family law specialist, it does not mean that he is good.

You also should consider choosing an attorney who works in the same county, if not the same town, where your case will be heard. The reasons for this are simple. First, chances are that if your attorney works in the same town or county, he has what is known as the "home court advantage." (When sports teams play on their home court, they always feel more empowered and more of their fans are there to cheer them on to victory.) It's the same on the legal court. The home court attorney may know the other attorneys in the courtroom and may even know the judge. He may be able to talk to the judge and relate to her in a way that a stranger could not. When possible, and when it makes sense, always go with the home court advantage. Second, if your attorney has to travel distances to appear in court on your case, you are going to pay extra fees.

If you are going to hire an attorney to collect child support money that's past due, your best bet would be to find a small law firm that specializes in the collection of debts. Attorneys who work for large firms usually will want to work with matters that can make them a lot of money or bring them a lot of prestige. Unless the amount of money owed to your child(ren) is in the mid- to high-five figures, at least, chances are that a large firm will not want to work with you since it will not be beneficial to them.

There are firms, however, that specifically hire collection attorneys—that is, attorneys who are trained to collect debts from people who owe money. Typically, these attorneys' clients are companies that are trying to collect past-due debts. After a few letters are sent requesting the money that is due, these companies send the bills to an attorney to collect the money for them. People who owe money will usually respond to a letter from an attorney because they are afraid of legal action. If they do not pay the bill immediately, the attorney can file a lawsuit against the person or company that owes the money.

Begin your search by locating your nearest bar association. To do this, visit your local library or call directory assistance. Depending on where you live, you may have a city or county bar association available to you. If so, contact them first. If not, try calling your state bar association. Every state has a bar association, but they may refer you to a regional office. Once you have contacted your nearest bar association, use their referral line to locate attorneys who specialize in general law, and also in child support cases. If they do not have any attorneys with that specialty, ask for attorneys who specialize in divorce or family law. But remember to ask for a child support attorney first, since not all divorce or family law attorneys know how to enforce a child support order. You also want attorneys who are willing to collect their fee from the non-custodial parent, or who are willing to place a *lien* on your property instead of receiving any up-front payments. Liens will be discussed in more detail in the next chapter.

There may not be any information listed with the bar association other than what type of law each attorney practices, but it's worth a try. Some bar associations have more information than others. If they do not have the information that you need, you may have to call each attorney to whom you are referred and ask each one yourself. The bar association will usually refer you to three or four attorneys at a time. They also may charge a fee, so ask them up front if they do, then decide if you still wish to use their service.

If you don't have any luck with the bar associations, check the Yellow Pages of your telephone directory under collection agencies. Call all of the collection agencies that are listed and tell them you would like the name of their collection attorney because you would like to hire him. When you have a list of at least ten attorneys, call them all. It's important to call more than just a few since some may not be willing to work with you, and those who will work with you will all charge different fees.

If you are unable to find an attorney through either of the previous methods, try calling small firms in your area that specialize in "general law." General law means that they are a jack-of-all-trades and will take any case as long as it will make them money and they believe that they can handle it. These small firms work well because they work hard, and it's cases like yours that are the meat and potatoes of their business. If they do not know something, generally they will persist until they get the information that they need to help you.

Once you've got an attorney on the phone, asking for references is a good way of judging whether he will be good for you or not. Ask for a list of three clients whom the attorney has already helped and be sure to speak with all three references. If you are not able to get into contact with them all, call the attorney back and ask for others.

When you call the references that the attorney has given to you, do not bother to ask if he was a good attorney. Chances are the reference was satisfied with the work that was done, or the attorney would not have given you the name in the first place. What you are going to ask will be more specific. Inquire about the procedures the attorney used and if he was a pleasure to work with or not. If the attorney you are considering uses mostly standard procedures and is not very innovative, he will not be a good choice for you. Likewise, if he operates in many of the ways that typically cause clients to be discontented with their attorneys, then you may want to continue to look. Ask if the attorney ever:

- Failed to return phone calls
- Failed to file documents on time
- Charged too much money
- Didn't follow through on what he had promised to do
- Was late for appointments or court dates

The best way to be referred to an attorney is through someone who has hired him before. If you know someone who has been divorced, ask if she liked her attorney and why. Find out if the attorney had any of the detrimental characteristics listed above.

Before you choose an attorney, you should have spoken with at least ten of them and gotten references on at least five. When you have at least three attorneys you liked over the phone, have checked their references, and it seems that you will be able to work with them, make appointments to meet with them. Now you are ready to interview. This is the last step before selecting the attorney that you will want to have work with you. Begin by writing down a list of questions that you will want to ask this attorney. When you meet with him be confident, professional, and relaxed. It may be helpful for you to bring a notebook with you, so you can jot down information that you want to remember. Here is a list of questions that you will want to ask any lawyer before you allow him to take your case:

1. Is he experienced with enforcing child support orders? You will want to know what methods he has used to get non-custodial parents to pay. There are many methods that can be used, so basically you are pressuring him to see how many he can name in about five to ten minutes. The next few chapters detail most of the methods. After you finish reading this book, you will know what to look for. Obviously, the attorney who is up to speed in terms of knowledge will be an attorney in whom you are interested.

2. Of course, you are still interested in financing your attorney. You will want to know: how much he charges, is there a consultation fee, does he want a *retainer*, will he work on a contingency fee, will he take a payment plan? The attorneys in whom you will be interested are the ones who will agree to work with you in some way. We will talk more about financing options later in the chapter.

3. Is he a subscriber to any *credit reporting agencies*? The attorney you select may need to use the credit reporting agencies to gather information about the non-custodial parent. A subscriber to the agencies pays a monthly fee to have access to credit reports, making it easier for the lawyer to get the information. A non-subscriber will have to pay another attorney a fee to get the information. Obviously, it will be easier and cheaper if he can get the information directly. There is more on how credit reports can be used to your advantage in Chapters 7 to 11.

4. Will he be willing to obtain liens and judgments against the non-custodial parent on your behalf? Is he familiar with how to have

a wage *execution* implemented? Will he issue subpoenas and conduct judgment debtor exams for you? (Do not worry about what these things mean right now, you will find out in the upcoming chapters.) Chances are you will get a few raised eyebrows when you ask these questions. The lawyer you will be interviewing will probably be wondering where you got all of this information. Of course, you will be able to answer intelligently any questions that he asks of you, because you will have read this entire book. If you cannot remember everything, bring the book with you. The important thing is that you are investigating to select the right attorney to handle your case. That will earn you some respect.

After you have met with your three prospective choices, choose the one you feel will best represent you and with whom you feel the most comfortable. If you find yourself with a bad attorney, fire him. Since you will have to pay him for services performed, it's best to do this sooner, rather than later. It is not uncommon for clients to switch attorneys in the middle of a case, so do not be ashamed to do it. Just call him and explain that you would like to have your case file forwarded to your new attorney. If you are asked for an explanation, you may give one if you so choose, but it is not required. If you are too uncomfortable making the call, your new attorney will be happy to do it for you.

Remember that you should have a good relationship with your attorney. You should not feel as if someone is putting you down or doing you a favor by taking your case. You are paying him good money to do a job. If you feel at any time during your interview that your chemistry is not right, or if you believe that this attorney is not capable of helping you, do not hire him.

Now that you know how to find and hire an attorney, you must be sure that you can pay him. Attorney fees vary from firm to firm and from state to state. Generally, you will be billed an hourly fee unless other arrangements are made in advance. If you do not have the money to pay an attorney up front for his services, you can try a little bit of "creative financing." Not all attorneys will go for this so it is up to you to express your enthusiasm and confidence in your case and why the attorney should be willing to work unconventionally. The following questions should be asked:

Question #1: Ask if he is willing to take the case on a contingency basis. Contingency means that if he does not collect any money for you, then he is not paid. Usually accident cases work this way. The law firm pays all the expenses that are necessary to try the case or get a settlement. When the money is recovered, they take a percentage of the total amount. The percentage that they take can vary greatly, but it is usually about a third of the total that is won. For example, if the child support amount that is outstanding is $10,000, then your attorney's law firm would end up with $3,333, and your child(ren) would get $6,667. That's a huge chunk of money to lose out on, so you would have to make the hard decision of whether it is worth it to you or not. Some people are of the opinion that it is not worth it since the money that is being lost rightfully belongs to their child(ren) and should not come out of their pocket. Others hold the position that if they are not getting any money for their children now and have had to go to an attorney to enforce their child support order, then chances are that unless some drastic action is taken, the child support money will never be recovered. In this instance, it is rationalized that a little bit of money is better than none at all. Only you, on behalf of your children, can make these difficult choices for your own family.

If you do find an attorney who is willing to take the case on a contingency basis, do not be surprised if he wants more than a third. You may be asked for 40 or 50 percent of what is owed. Why? Because the attorney knows you are in a difficult position and may have nowhere else to turn. Another reason a lawyer may charge a lot is because child support cases can be difficult to work. Only you can decide if it's worth it to you. Also note that a contingency arrangement may be problematic if you choose to change attorneys midstream. Who gets what may be an area of contention between the two attorneys.

Question #2: Another option you have is to ask if the law firm is willing to put you on a payment plan to work off the debt you owe to them. Attorneys are often willing to make these types of arrangements.

The key to whether either of these options may work for you is the amount of child support that is past due. Obviously, if you go to an attorney and ask for a contingency plan when your child(ren) are owed $3,000 in past-due child support, the plan would not work for you in most cases. The law firm in this case would only stand to make $1,000. While $1,000 may be a lot to some people, the average attorney would scoff at that amount considering the headaches that must be endured while attempting to collect the money. And, they only get paid if they are successful. Also consider the part of the country that you live in. In the Northeast, $1,000 does not get you very far, while in the Midwest, the value is much greater.

After you have discussed contingency fees and payment plans and are making an appointment to see your potential attorney, there are a few more questions you should ask before you end your conversation. Find out if you will be charged a consultation fee for the time that it takes to meet with you. Some attorneys charge consultation fees and you need to know this before you make your appointment. If they do charge such a fee, you need to know how much. Some law firms also require a retainer. A retainer is a fee paid to an attorney when the client (that's you) hires him. It's a deposit that is applied toward the fees that you will be charged.

If you are really strapped for cash, as most custodial parents are, especially when they are not getting child support, you may not be able to pay anything to an attorney. It is an option to consider if you have money to lay out. Let's move on to how you can find an attorney to work for you for little or no money at all!

chapter 6

finding a free attorney

After reading Chapter 5, "Finding and Hiring an Attorney," you now know that there are some creative ways of paying your attorney once you decide to hire him. The attorney you choose has to be agreeable to it, of course. You will now learn ways of getting an attorney to work for you for absolutely nothing at all. Absolutely nothing out of your pocket, that is, and that's what we are concerned about, right?

Nothing is free. But, this does not mean that you have to be the one who pays. If you have tried to hire a private attorney but cannot afford one the conventional way, and you have not found one who will work with you creatively concerning payment, you can try legal aid, government attorneys, and/or having the non-custodial parent pay the attorney fees.

legal aid

Attorneys are available for custodial parents who are trying to get child support from an absent parent. Usually, every county in every state will have an office to serve you. If you do not know where the legal aid office in your area is, you may:

• Look it up in your telephone directory. In the White Pages, search for a listing under legal aid. In the Yellow Pages, look under both "attorneys" and "lawyers" and then search for any listing under legal aid. Be sure to look for advertisments as well. You can also check the Blue Pages under government agencies in your county. A telephone number for legal aid may be listed there.

• Call directory assistance (information) and ask for the legal aid office in your county. In most areas an information call will cost more money than a regular local call would. If you do not want to pay the extra money because you are on a tight budget, as most custodial parents are, use a public pay phone to place the information call. Most pay phones will not charge you for an information call. Then go home and place the local call from your home telephone.

• Call your local welfare department or child support enforcement agency. Tell them that you are searching for your county's legal aid office. Generally, they should be able to help you.

• Your local library has a wealth of information. Call or visit the reference desk and let the reference librarian know that you need to find the legal aid office for your area. If anyone can find the number and address in a flash, the reference librarian can.

• Finally, some law schools run legal aid programs that serve the public. If there are any law schools in your area, find out if they provide these services.

In order to use the services of the legal aid office you must be either indigent or have an income that is considered to be at or below the poverty level for where you live. If you are on welfare, you will automatically qualify for services. If you have a job but make very little money, you need to find out what the poverty level is in your area to know whether or not you qualify. A large number of people fall into a gray area that is sometimes difficult to determine. There are some people who may be on welfare, or not have a job, they may not be getting child support for their children, but because they own the house that they live in, they will not qualify for free legal services. Some people do not have any source of income, and are not receiving court-ordered child support or alimony, yet they have been forced to leave their homes with their children because they can no longer afford the upkeep. They still may not be qualified for legal aid because they are still married to their spouse who is a high earner. Therefore, it is thought that they do not need handouts. There are many situations such as these where custodial parents are turned down for legal assistance even though they have no money of their own.

If this sounds like your situation, you must prepare your financial statement before your appointment with the legal aid office. Use the chart that is available to you in Chapter 1, "Establishing Your Child Support Order." It will help you to outline what your expenses are. You will also need to provide the legal aid office with information on all of your income, including child support and alimony, if you get any. You need to show that even though you may have a spouse who makes a great deal of money, he does not give you any. Bring your overdue bills, eviction notices, and whatever else you have to plead your case. Although the legal aid office has guidelines that they follow when they accept clients, they will make their own final decision.

When you use the services of the legal aid office, if it is shown that you have no money to pay your bill, as in the case of indigence, you will receive the services free of charge. If it is thought that you are not completely indigent, you may be asked to pay a reduced fee. Normally this is billed on a sliding scale according to your income. The more money you make, the more you will be charged, up to the normal fee that others pay. The less money you make, the less you will be charged. If the only reason you are not considered indigent is due to possession of property rather than income, ask if the legal aid office will place a lien on your property.

A lien is a claim upon property that prevents its sale or transfer until a debt is satisfied. Legally, no one (not you, your husband, or any outside party) could sell your property until the debt to legal aid had been paid. In other words, you, or whoever received payment for the property, would have to subtract the amount of the debt from the payment, which would go to legal aid. If the sale somehow did go through without the debt being paid, the lien would still be attached to the property so that the debt now would be the responsibility of the new owner of the property. The idea is that legal aid is guaranteed its money when you actually have it on hand, and in the meantime you have the help you need.

If you are planning to use the services of a legal aid office, keep in mind that they usually have a long waiting list. If you qualify for free or reduced rate services, put your name on the waiting list anyway. If something else comes up in the meantime, and you are able to get an attorney by other means, then it's just gravy for you. You need to have as many choices as you can. Do not worry about not needing their services when your time comes—it will be easy for them to go on to the next person on the list.

government attorneys

Government attorneys are free to anyone and everyone who wants to use them—with a few catches, however. They are usually referred to as Title IV-D attorneys because they work for the *Title IV-D agencies*. Title IV-D agencies are the child support enforcement agencies in every county that are bound by law to help you enforce your child support order. This is the office that you visit when you open your child support case. If you have a case that is easy to manage, the caseworker to whom you have been assigned may be the only person with whom you have contact. If your case is in need of more legwork—if the non-custodial parent needs to be located, or if you need a *wage withholding*, etc.—a government attorney will have to be the one to handle these matters for you. The attorney will only become involved if certain services need to be implemented. The attorney is free and is available to anyone who has a case in a Title IV-D agency. This is not an attorney whom you can call up and hire as you would any other. They are sheltered and protected by the agency because there are not many of them. They have an over-whelming caseload and have a difficult time keeping up with the many cases that they are assigned. Frankly, publicizing their exis-tence is sure to cause problems for them and a longer waiting list for you. The reason I am willing to cause such a ruckus is because no one at the agency will tell you about them unless they are forced to do so. This does not help you in the least bit. What does help you is knowing that there are things that these attorneys can do that can make a world of difference to your child support case. They will be covered in more detail in Chapter 11, "What the Government Can Do for You".

As with any other attorney or other goods or services that you can get for free, it will not be made easy for you. First, you must again put yourself on the waiting list, or at least let it be known that you want and need the services of these attorneys. You will be fully prepared after reading this entire book to inform the attorney of what services you feel will work well with your case. You can then ask if they have any further suggestions. You will be attempting to build a relationship with this attorney so that the two of you can work together to enforce your child support order. One bit of caution: since these are government attorneys, they work for the government and they do not work for you. Uncle Sam hires them to help collect on cases in which the government is particularly interested. If you are on welfare, the government is supporting you so it has a direct interest in whether you get your child support or not. Every child support case of those who are on welfare is handled by the state collection agencies—the Title IV-D child support enforcement offices to which I have been referring. If you have read the introduction to this book, you know that when these agencies were opened in 1974 the government decided to give the same services to anyone who had a child support case. So even though these attorneys' primary interest is not in helping the non-welfare cases, they will. Just remember that they do not work directly for you. It will be awfully difficult to fire them and you may not want to since they have the means to help you. One more final word—anything you share with them will be shared with the government as well. There will not be any client confidentiality in your relationship as far as the government is concerned. Also, you will be sharing your attorney with many others. If the non-custodial parent of your child has another child with some-one else, you may have to share your attorney with her as well.

If you contact your local office for assistance from a government attorney, you are likely to get one or more of these responses:

- You may be told to retain a private attorney.
- You may be discouraged from seeking assistance from a government attorney due to a long waiting list.
- You may be told that you cannot contact the government attorney—he will contact you.
- You may be told that there aren't any government attorneys.
- People may be rude to you and not help you at all.

If you get any of these responses, and chances are very good that you will, do not let them confuse or anger you. Read on—in Chapter 20, "Effective Complaining," you will learn how to deal with these issues.

non-custodial parent pays attorney fees

If you must take the non-custodial parent to court to collect your child support, you can normally collect attorney fees from him. If, after reading this entire book, you decide that it may be in your best interest to go to court, you will possibly be in a better position to hire an attorney without any payment from you. Most judges will award attorney fees to the *plaintiff* (that's you) and attorneys know this. The drawback is that the amount awarded to you may be significantly lower than the fee you will be charged. This is where some more cre-ative financing may have to come into play. Your attorney may not ask you for the remainder of the bill, but if he does you will be responsible for it.

The non-custodial parent may scoff at your attorney bill. If you are not able to collect child support, chances are that you will not be able to get this bill paid either. On the other hand, after appearing in court the non-custodial parent may come to his senses. Maybe, or maybe not. This advice may not help all custodial parents but it will give some of you another option, and for others it will actually work. If it does not help you, just press on. At the very least, you have just added more money onto the bill that the non-custodial parent cannot run away from forever. For now—maybe. Forever—never.

chapter 7

locating the obligor

When I was a girl of about ten, I read mystery novels in which a teenage sleuth would solve problems in her town. I was fascinated with how the young detective would have the smallest clues and yet was able to solve her mysteries. This chapter reminds me of my childhood with that young detective. Most custodial parents with child support orders will find that, at some point, they may need to search for either the non-custodial parent or his assets, or sometimes both. The least of offenders may move to a different town or county or maybe take a new job and not advise you. This makes it difficult to get money from him. The greater offenders will go through a lot more trouble. It is not uncommon for those who owe child support (obligors) to move to a new state. They may also put all of their assets into a new spouse's name, lie and cheat on tax documents, and more, all in order to avoid paying child support. That is why this chapter was written. Countless child support cases are left untouched in the child support agencies, simply because the caseworkers do not have enough information. They cannot find the obligors or they believe that they do not have jobs or that they earn far less than they actually do. Unless they have more information, their hands are tied. If you want your child support, you may have to put on your own detective cap and get to work. Information that can be used to track someone down is abundant, you just have to know where to look.

When I was in college and had my first apartment, I worked at a bank collecting on loans that were past due. Frequently, I had accounts where the customer skipped town without paying the bill. These accounts were called "skips." Part of my job was to perform preliminary "skip tracing" on these accounts before they were sent to our legal department. During my employment at that bank, I was honored for being the "Collector of the Month" in my department every month that I was there. I will now share some of my secrets with you.

The first thing you want to do is gather as much information about the obligor as you can. If you lived with him you may have more information at your disposal than someone who did not. If you are still living with the obligor, or have access to his personal financial information, you are ahead of the game. Photocopy whatever paperwork you can, especially income tax records for the past three to five years and the obligor's Social Security Number. Brainstorm for any information that you can come up with. When you are done, get paper and a pen to list the following data:

1. What is the obligor's full name? Has he ever used any other names? Does he have any nicknames?

2. What is the obligor's birth date? Where was he born?

3. What is the obligor's Social Security Number?

4. What is the most recent address that you have for the obligor?

5. List the addresses at which the obligor has lived for the past three years.

6. What is the most recent telephone number that you have for the obligor?

7. Where does the obligor work? Write down the name of the company as well as the address and telephone number. Do you know his supervisor's or manager's name? Write it down. What does the obligor do for a living? What is his title?

8. List the obligor's employers for the past three years, as well as their addresses and phone numbers. Also list the supervisor or manager. Was he employed in the same capacity as he is now?

9. If the obligor is self-employed, list the clients that he has had for the past three years. If you have their addresses and/or telephone numbers, list those as well.

10. What is the obligor's driver's license number, and which state issued it? What is the make, model, and year of the vehicle that he drives? What is the plate number and the vehicle identification number?

11. Has the obligor been formerly married? If so, list all former marriages including the dates of the marriage and dissolution. List the former spouse's maiden name and employment history as well.

12. List the names and addresses of the obligor's parents, including the obligor's mother's maiden name. If they still work, what are their occupations and where are they employed?

13. List the obligor's siblings and friends along with their addresses, telephone numbers, and employment info.

14. List the obligor's creditors.

15. List the obligor's bank and insurance company.

16. List any real estate that the obligor owns.

17. Does the obligor belong to any clubs or organizations? List them.

18. What hobbies does the obligor have?

19. Does the obligor vote? If so, where is he registered and for what party?

20. Does the obligor receive, or will the obligor receive in the future, any military, government, or private pension or other benefits?

21. List any military service of the obligor. Include the branch of service, dates and locations of assignment, rank, service number, date, and status of discharge.

22. If the obligor has ever been in prison, list the conviction(s) including the date and location of conviction, the offense, and the location of incarceration.

23. If the obligor is or has ever been on probation, list the state and county and the name of the probation officer.

24. Is the obligor presently married? If so, assemble all of the aforementioned information on his spouse as well.

Along the way you will undoubtedly uncover other information that you could not put your hands on or did not know about the obligor from the start. Add what you find out to your reference. The more that you know about your obligor, the better your chances are of locating him. It's like a game of hide and seek. Your obligor is hiding and you're going to find him. Now that you have your completed list I will tell you how to use it. Ready?

Come out, come out, wherever you are!

telephone directories

The simplest way to locate anyone is through a telephone directory. Although it may sound foolish—why on earth would anyone who is trying to hide have a listed telephone number—it's not uncommon. So just to be certain that you are covering all of your bases, you should also call the directory assistance in your area. Ask for the obligor by name in the city in which you last knew him to live. Be sure also to check under any other names that the obligor may be using. Every name that the obligor has ever used is suspect. If you are able to get a telephone number, ask if there is an address listed as well. Some information directories will give you an address if they have one, some will not. In some areas there is an address directory that can be used if you have a telephone number. It is an automated system that is used by punching in the telephone number of the person for whom you would like to have an address. If the person has given permission for his address to be publicly listed, you will be given the address that they have available. For example, in the New York Metropolitan area, the number for the address directory is 555-5454. Ask the telephone information bureau in your area if there is such a service that you can use.

Most likely you will get one of these two responses:

1. You may find that there is a listing for your obligor, but that the telephone number is not available to the public. If this is the response that you are given, press on. You will be able to utilize other methods in this chapter to locate an address now that you know that the obligor is in town.

2. There is also the possibility that you will get a listed number and call it only to find that the number you received has been reassigned

to someone else and that it is not a correct number after all. The smallest possibility remains that you could actually get a real working number for the obligor, but let's not bet the bank on it.

backward directories

When I was working in collections, there were times when we were able to find a current telephone number for an obligor, but no address. Conversely, maybe we had an address, but no telephone number. When this situation occurred we had special directories to help us out. There are several companies that publish or print these directories. In our office we used "Coles" directories and "backward" directories. They are backward listings of telephone numbers and addresses. In these directories you can look up a person's telephone number and find his or her address. Likewise, you can use an address to find a telephone number. These directories can be found at your local library, and the reference librarian should be able to show you how to use them. If your library doesn't have them because it is too small to stock such items, go to the largest library in your area—it will be sure to carry at least one brand. Also available are city directories at the local Chamber of Commerce. These city directories give the same information, with one additional plus: it may also state the found person's occupation and place of employment. City directories are mainly used to obtain current addresses for the service of legal documents. Since that is what you need it for, it should work perfectly for you.

These directories will also provide names, addresses, and telephone numbers of neighbors or former neighbors of the obligor. Continue on with this chapter and you will find out why this information can be helpful to you.

post office

It used to be very easy to get information from the post office. Years ago, anyone could walk into a post office and get the forwarding address of someone who had moved. In fact it was far too easy. Men who beat up, threatened, and stalked their wives and girlfriends could easily get this information and follow an ex to a new address and continue the same patterns of abuse. Because of this, the Domestic Violence Act was put into place. You can no longer get information from the post office unless you have a valid legal reason for having it, and you must be able to prove that you need the new address to serve legal documents on the person you are seeking.

Your first step is to obtain a judgment against the obligor. If you have already been to court and have received a court order for child support but the obligor is not paying, that is enough. When someone at the post office asks for proof that you will be serving legal documents, supply your child support order and the motion that you will be serving. Having a judgment is the easiest way to prove that you have a valid legal reason to have the obligor's new address. If you need the address to take the obligor to court for the first time, your task becomes a bit more difficult. There is almost no way to prove that you will be using the address within the realms of the law. You may have to serve him or her "by publication." This is described later in this chapter.

If you are able to prove that you have legal reasons for needing the obligor's address, you can request the information two ways:

1. The easiest and the fastest way to get the information you need is to go directly to the post office in the area where the obligor last received mail. Bring your documentation with you and expect to pay

a small fee of about $5. The postal clerk will give you a "Freedom of Information" form to fill out. The clerk will then do an immediate search and give you the obligor's new address on the spot.

2. If you are unable to go to the post office, you can ask that a Freedom of Information form be mailed to you. You can then fill it out, attach your documentation, and the appropriate fee, and mail it back to the post office. You should receive a reply by mail within about thirty days.

If the obligor was receiving mail at a post office box, the postal clerk will be able to get the address from the application that the obligor completed when the box was rented. If the post office box was rented under a business name the information contained on the application is considered to be public knowledge. You will not have to prove legal reasons for wanting the renter's address, so you can get this information by visiting the post office, by mail, and even over the telephone.

Often you will find that deadbeat obligors move around quite a bit. Even if you have received a new address, that doesn't guarantee the obligor still lives there. If you want to know up front whether the obligor still lives at the address that the post office is supplying to you, simply add to your form another line: addressee still receives mail at this address, with a check line for yes and a check line for no. The postal clerk will then check the appropriate line and you will have your answer. If the answer is no, you will have to continue sending forms to the post offices that serve each new address until you are provided with one that is current.

You may run into a postal clerk who tells you that under no circumstances can you or will you be provided with the information that you are requesting. At that time you must ask to speak with the postmaster. She is head honcho at the post office and every station has one. The postmaster will be more familiar than a postal clerk with what can or cannot be done legally. If you have a problem with the postmaster, simply get her information and write a letter stating what you are asking for and why. Supply your proof of a need for legal service and ask for assistance. After receiving your letter, the post-master may then realize that you mean business and that you are not going away. If she is unfamiliar with the law, most likely she will decide to take the time to find out the facts. A small suggestion that you may consider legal action for being denied your right to this information may cause her to think twice before again turning you down. I do caution you not to make threats on which you can't fol-low through. If you don't get anywhere with the post office, you have other options available to you.

voter registration records

If your obligor is civic-minded, he may be a registered voter. If you move from the area where you initially registered to become a voter, you must re-register in the new area. Most registration offices require that you submit valid current identification when you reg-ister. If you have located a town or a city but cannot find a street address for your obligor, this may be a good source for you. All voter registration information is open to the public and may also contain political party affiliation as well as a date of birth and occupation.

utility company records

Utility companies can be a good source of information. If your obligor skipped town but is still in the state somewhere, this could be your gold mine. When most people move but stay within the same state, they transfer their utility service to their new location. Utility companies are not supposed to give out this information, but they do all the time. The best way to get information may be to fib about why you want it in the first place. I've always found it useful to assume the identity of a more-than-helpful delivery person. It doesn't matter what company you pretend to be with—you can make one up if you want to. The important thing is that you play your part well. Your premise is that you are calling the utility company because John Doe ordered some merchandise from you that was on back order. The merchandise has just come in and you attempted to deliver it but the package was returned because he has moved and you do not know where he lives now. Could they please supply the current address so that you can re-deliver the merchandise? It's as simple as that. If the first customer service representative will not give you the address, hang up and call back. Keep calling until you get someone who will help you. If you get the same representative twice, hang up. You don't want him or her to flag the account for the next person to see. Refine and perfect your story with each call that you make. If being a delivery person is not your bag, you can be a nurse from John Doe's doctor's office calling with test results and you urgently need to speak with him. Be creative and have fun with it. Sooner or later you will hit pay dirt.

department of motor vehicles records

The department of motor vehicles in all states used to provide information the same way that the post office did in the past. But because of the Domestic Violence Act, they too are limiting with whom they share information. As of this writing, there are several states that are prohibiting the release of driver and registration record information. The exception to this rule is, of course, if you are an attorney or a member of law enforcement.

Look up the number for the motor vehicle department in your state in the phone book and call and ask what their policy is. You may find that your state will provide information as a matter of public record. In this case, you will need to write a letter requesting the information, including the driver's full name, most recent address known, date of birth, and Social Security Number if you have it. There is a small fee involved as well, usually about $5. The motor vehicle department will respond to you in writing with the requested information. Be sure to call both the department of driver's records and the department of registration records. They are separate departments and may have different records on the obligor.

If someone at the motor vehicle department says that she will not supply the information to you, send the letter anyway. Who knows if the person you spoke with is up-to-date with policies? Also remember that if you have proof that you need a current address in order to serve legal documentation you will probably get more help.

Once you receive an address from motor vehicles, be sure to verify it through the post office to be sure that it is current. If the obligor's driving record indicates that he has received tickets or has had accidents, this may indicate the area where he spends a lot of time.

neighbors

Former neighbors are another good source of information. If the obligor is no longer living at the last address known to you, use the city directory to get telephone numbers of his former neighbors. The city directory will provide you with the address and telephone number of the person for whom you are searching as well as the same information for the people that live nearby. If the obligor lived in an apartment building, you will find names, addresses, and telephone numbers of other people who live in the same building. If he lived in a house, you will find names, addresses, and telephone numbers for the people who lived next door, down the block, across the street, etc. You could take this as far as you want.

Call them with the same delivery person technique. It works great with neighbors. You would be surprised at the amount of information an unsuspecting neighbor will regurgitate if you sound sincere enough. Good neighbors are always willing to help other good neighbors. If you find that your obligor was not a good neighbor at all, then you should be truthful about who you are and what you are trying to do. Your obligor's former neighbor will likely be pleased to help you catch your bandit. Pump them for whatever you can get.

former landlords

The best former landlords to find will be the ones where the obligor skipped out owing rent. They will be happy to help, especially if you tell them that you will relay to them information on the whereabouts of the obligor once he is found. If your obligor left on good terms with the landlord, then you may not be able to talk them into giving you private information on one of their former tenants. Subpoena any information that you might need from an unyielding former landlord. They may have details that the obligor listed on their rental application that will be helpful to you. If you are lucky enough to find the landlord before they refund a security deposit to the obligor, you can garnish the refund. Chapter 9 covers *garnishments*.

former employers

Former employers are similar to former landlords in that if the obligor was a horrible employee and caused nothing but problems, the employer may be willing to provide you with whatever information will be helpful. If the obligor left on suitable terms, you can forget about the employer being helpful to you at all, with the exception of the subpoena, of course.

clients

If the obligor is self-employed and you know who some of his clients are, they, too, will be able to provide information on the whereabouts of the obligor. Certainly clients know how to get in contact with someone who is providing a service to them! Not only that, but they will also be able to fill you in on how much money they supplied to the obligor over the past year—or longer if they have an ongoing relationship. If they were provided with references before they did business with the obligor, the references will be able to help you as well. The biggest bonus, though, is the humiliation that the obligor will suffer when his clients confront him about the subpoenas they've received from someone who is trying to collect child support. Humiliation may be enough to cause the obligor to want to pay you so that it doesn't happen again. Whatever works is to your advantage, and causing your obligor some humiliation can be quite satisfying.

career licenses

What does the obligor do for a living? Is he a doctor, lawyer, Indian chief, or anything else that requires a license? If so, check with the source of where he must be licensed and you may find current address information. Most licensing bureaus have detailed information that is available to the public. The address that you find may be a business address, not a home address, but it's better than not finding anything at all. The obligor does not need to be at home to be served. An obligor can be served at a business address. Is he a plumber, stock trader, trucker, or an insurance agent? All of these must be licensed. Maybe the obligor works for a supermarket and belongs to a union. Trade unions should have information as well.

obligors in the military

Did your obligor join the military? While enlisted, did he get shipped off to some foreign country, and you now have no idea where he is? Collecting from military employees can be difficult, so there is an entire chapter focused on just that. For our purposes in this chapter, however, you should know that there are special military locators available through the government for a fee. Should you decide to take that route, see Chapter 16, "Collecting from Military Personnel," for more information.

alumni associations

Alumni associations keep current addresses on graduates for informational purposes so they can send invitations to reunion parties and requests for donations . Dream up a good enough reason and they, too, will tell you whatever they know.

hobbies

Does the obligor ride a bike? If so, has he ever had a bike permit? If the answer is yes, he may have a permit in the town in which he lives. Does the obligor enjoy hunting or other similar sports? He may have filed a gun, fishing, or hunting license. These licenses are all a matter of public record in most areas.

family and friends

Surely you must know some of the obligor's family and friends. Contact them for information. Start by trying to appeal to their good conscience. Let them know that child support is something that your children need. They may not budge to help you one bit. Or they may want to help you but feel that they will be betraying a family member or friend if they do. Start by asking, but if they don't tell you anything, you can rely on the subpoena. It's like a magic wand. Wave it around in someone's face and—poof!—like magic you get what you want. Of course, you will want to start your inquisitions with the family members or friends whom the obligor has stiffed in some way. They will be the ones most likely to spill the beans.

other government records

If the obligor owns a business, it should be registered with the state somewhere. Check corporation records, partnership, and assumed business records (DBA) with the secretary of the state in which the obligor lives. An assumed business name is a business name that a company has chosen to operate under, even though their legal business name may be something else. An assumed business name must be registered with the state. This information can be given over the telephone. Does the business that the obligor operates collect any sales tax? If so, it must have a license and this information is available to the public. There are other licenses you should check out, such as: a dog license, a parking permit, a sign permit, a fire permit, or a vending permit.

real estate tax records

If the obligor owns any real property, he will be listed with the county, along with the property owned, the amount of taxes paid, and the most current address known. This information is all public knowledge and can be obtained over the telephone.

criminal records

If the obligor has been in trouble with the law, the county where the offense occurred will have a good deal of information on him. Contact the probation or parole officer, if there is one, and get information from that source. The more recent the violation, the more recent the information that you receive will be. If the violation is an old one, it will only be useful to make contact if you are searching for a Social Security Number or perhaps the name of family or friends. Any other information will most likely be outdated.

other court records

Has the obligor recently divorced, or is he divorcing? Has he recently been sued or is he suing anyone? All of these matters are public records and any information that you cannot get immediately, you can subpoena.

the internet

Computers are the tree of life and the Internet is its ripe delicious fruit, ready for the picking. As with conventional methods, the Internet provides many ways for you to locate someone who has skipped out on you. It is not foolproof, but it can provide information that might have taken a lot of research for you to find on your own.

At the same time, sometimes doing things the slow and steady way wins the race, since the Internet cannot provide everything. Also keep in mind that this is just computerized information, and if the information put into the system is bad, the information coming out is also bad. Don't rely solely on the Internet, it is just one of many tools that you have at your disposal.

Begin by trying one of the well-known directories, such as www.800seachusa.com, www.bigyellow.com, or www.four11.com. These directories can give you information on people that is listed in the White Pages of their local phone book. Of course, if they are trying not to be found, they most likely will not be listed, but you never know.

A good directory is www.peoplefinder.excite.com. Not only will you be provided with an address and telephone number if you get a "hit," but you will also get an email address, business name and address, and an employer if one is listed. You provide peoplefinder with whatever information you have, whether it is a name, address, or phone number, and if a "hit" is made, peoplefinder will provide you with the rest.

If you don't have any luck with the preceding sources, you can look for others on your own. Simply go to a search engine like Yahoo (www.yahoo.com) and type in: find people. You will get a listing of resources like the ones I have mentioned.

If you don't mind paying and have the ability to pay, there are also peoplefinders that will locate your lost lamb for a fee. They claim to have about a 95 percent hit rate. While that may sound promising, usually they charge you a fee for the search even if they don't get a "hit" for you. So you may end up paying something for nothing. These services charge in the range of thirty to fifty dollars for a basic search. The more that you want them to find for you, the more that they will charge.

The keys to finding someone on the Internet are:

1. Experiment with variations and alternate spellings of names. If you are looking for John, also try Johnathan, Jonathan, and Jon.

2. Start with just one initial and then add more letters to your search if you need to—his name may be misspelled in the directory, intentionally or not. Try J. Smith instead of John Smith. Proceed to Jo, then Joh, etc.

3. Does John have a middle name? I have known people who chose to list their phone number using their middle name rather than their first name to save the $1.50 per month the phone company charges for an unlisted number. What would stop anyone else from doing the same to avoid being easily found? Try J. Edward Smith or Edward Smith or J.E. Smith.

4. The obligor may also be using an alternate name or a nick-name. If you are looking for Bill, try Billy, William, or Will. Don't forget that you must also then try Billy, William, and Will with alter-nate spellings and middle names, as well.

5. My first name is Simone, but I can't count the times that I have received mail addressed to Simon. Names can be misspelled and can "sound like" something else. Consider all of the possibilities.

6. Also remember that the obligor can have phone records and all other records listed under his new partner's name, his mother's name, his best friend's name, or his business name, etc.

credit reports

Credit reports are one of the most valuable tools available to you. It is difficult to operate in today's society without some type of credit or without someone checking your credit-worthiness for evaluation. Through a credit report you can get the most current address available, employment and asset information, as well as details on the obligor's credit history and financial standing. In short, you can get everything you need to declare war. The one obstacle you have will be finding someone who will run a credit report on the obligor for you. As a judgment creditor you have a legal right to this information, but the credit bureaus will not give it to you. Unless you operate a company that extends credit to consumers or you are an attorney, you are plumb out of luck. That is, of course, unless you have friends in high places who will get a copy of the report for you, or unless you hire someone to obtain one for you. If you don't mind waiting forever, using a government attorney through the state child support agency is the simplest way to get one since they are familiar with this practice and obtain reports on obligors frequently. If you do mind waiting forever, contact several attorneys who specialize in collections until you find one who will be willing to run a report for you—for a fee, of course. If you have decided to hire an attorney, hopefully you have already found one who has this capability. Once you have the report, call the credit bureau and ask for help interpreting it.

locator services

The child support agencies have two locator services available to them. One is the *State Parent Locator Service (SPLS)* and the other is the *Federal Parent Locator Service (FPLS)*. Custodial parents on AFDC can use these services without charge, all others are customarily charged a fee of approximately $10, with a maximum fee set at $25, although the state often absorbs all or most of the cost.

The state locator service is a computer network that will check all state records available in an effort to locate the obligor. If unsuccessful, the file will be sent to the federal service, which will conduct a search of federal records. If the federal locator is unable to locate the obligor, it is legally bound to try the search again every three months for three years.

Having the government conduct the search for you through all of its means sounds like a great idea. But all that glitters is not gold. The state locator has seventy-five days to complete the search and report back to you with a hit or miss. If the file is forwarded to a federal service, the time it takes to get back to you can vary. In the time it can take to complete all the government searches, you and your children may starve—this process often takes a year or longer. This is why you may need to take matters into your own hands at times.

When you visit your state agency to request a locator service, you will be asked to fill out a "registration of absent or punitive parents" and pay the fee requested. Ask at that time to have the state and the federal locator service run concurrently to save you some time and headaches. It is a common practice to exhaust the resources of the state locator before running the federal, but it does not have to be done that way. You may be told that if you are not on welfare or if you are not receiving the services of the state agency that you cannot apply for locator services, but that is untrue. Press on and insist that the caseworker check the guidelines. Anyone who requests this service is entitled to it as long as the fee is paid.

private investigators

If you are thinking of hiring a private investigator, there are some guidelines you should follow so that no one takes advantage of you.

• Decide how much money you are willing to spend and don't let the investigator talk you into spending any more. Include the investigator's expenses in this amount since they are not included in the fee quoted to you. You may decide that an investigator is too costly.

• Get an agreement on what expenses you will be expected to pay for and get it in writing.

• Get an agreement on what the hourly rates are and get it in writing.

• Ask for an accounting of the investigator's time and expenses.

• Ask how the investigation will be conducted. Fieldwork will be a lot less cost efficient than telephone work.

• Put the entire agreement in writing.

• Ask for at least three references who can recommend him based on his skip tracing abilities.

• Agree on written progress reports and ask that you receive them frequently.

• In your agreement, be sure to have a clause where you can terminate the investigator at any time, with a full refund on any unused retainers, if you are not happy with the service.

• If you do terminate your investigator, do not have any further contact with him until you receive your refund. He may charge you for whatever conversation you have and then tell you that you have no money left to refund.

service by publication

When all else fails and you are unable to locate the absent parent to serve him with legal papers, the law allows you to "serve by publication." This means that you must place an advertisement in the newspaper where the obligor is last known to have lived, announcing that he is being sued for child support. The advertisement must appear in the section where legal notices are posted and must include all of the pertinent information. This is a common practice and is allowable by law. You must get the judge's permission to serve the absent parent/obligor by publication. To do this you must file a motion with the court and ask the judge to sign it. Ask the clerk's office if they have pre-printed forms. If they do not, visit the office supply store nearest you and get one there. Item #4 is the motion that you need.

When filing your motion, you must attach an affidavit (a signed written statement) that states how you have attempted to otherwise serve the obligor and that you have been unsuccessful. You must also provide proof of your previous attempts of service.

MOTION AND ORDER TO ALLOW
SERVICE BY PUBLICATION

IN THE CIRCUIT COURT OF THE STATE OF [STATE NAME]
FOR THE COUNTY OF [COUNTY NAME]

In the Matter of .	)	
	)	No. 0000
[YOUR NAME],	)	
Petitioner	)	
	)	
and	)	
[OBLIGOR'S NAME],	)	MOTION AND ORDER
Respondent	)	TO ALLOW SERVICE
	)	BY PUBLICATION

[Your Name], petitioner in the above-captioned matter, hereby moves the Court for an order allowing Service by Publication.

This motion is based upon the attached affidavit, which is incorporated herein by reference.

_____
[YOUR NAME]
Petitioner

ORDER

IT IS SO ORDERED.

DATED this _____ day of _____, 20___.

_____
CIRCUIT COURT JUDGE

Item #4: Motion and Order to Allow Service By Publication

chapter 8

locating assets

If you have located the obligor, the next step is to find his assets so that you can take them and cash them in. Using many of the same methods that you used to locate the obligor, you can locate his assets. The only difference is that the first time you were looking for a current address of the obligor so that you could serve him legal papers, and now you are looking for income, or assets that you can convert into income. Contrary to popular belief, income is not only what a person earns. *Unearned income*, or income that is not earned through a paycheck, is considered to be income as well. Examples may include rental incomes, dividends and interest from stock ownership, etc. Virtually everything that belongs to the obligor can be construed as income or converted into income for your usage. You just have to know where to look and what to look for.

credit reports

As you have found in Chapter 7, credit reports can reveal an enormous amount of information that can be helpful to you. They can help you to locate an obligor who has skipped out on you. They can also help you find out what he owns. If you do not have access to a credit reporting system, find someone who does and pay to have a report run on the obligor for you, as described in Chapter 7.

This is what you will be looking for:

• If you haven't done so already, confirm the home address that's listed on the credit report with the post office. Next, find out if the obligor owns the home that he lives in. If he does, consider the option of placing a *judgment lien* (a lien that is enforced by a court order) on the property and threaten to force a foreclosure on the property unless you are paid in full. See Chapter 9 for more details.

• Does the obligor own any other real estate? Again, consider the option of forcing a foreclosure on the property.

• Does the obligor own cars, boats, motorcycles, or anything else that's valuable? If possible, drive by his house and assess the situation. Consider the option of filing a Writ of Execution with the court so that you can have the property seized and sold at auction. See Chapter 9 for more details.

If the obligor does not own the property where he lives, find out who does—you learned how to do this in Chapter 7. Subpoena the landlord to discover whether the obligor has a security deposit or not. If he does, file a Writ of Garnishment to have the money released to you. See Chapter 9 for details. A savvy landlord may decide to contest the garnishment contending that he is a lienholder on the account. Most people, including landlords, don't contest garnishments—they don't know that they can. If they do contest it, there is no guarantee that the judge will stop the garnishment from going through. If the judge will not stop the garnishment, the money is yours and the obligor will have to come up with another security deposit. If the judge does stop it, at the very least you can file a judgment lien against the deposit. When the obligor moves from the apartment, the money will be refunded to you as long as he does not owe anything to the landlord. If he does move owing money and the deposit is awarded to the landlord, at least you tried. Better luck on the next attack.

If the credit report reveals a current employer, you can have the obligor's wages withheld and/or garnished if you haven't done so already. See Chapter 9 for details.

When you contact the employer, ask if the obligor receives any bonuses or commissions. Also ask if he has any company savings plans or deductions such as an IRA or a 401K. Does he own any company stock? Does he have a pension plan? These items can all be considered income for the purposes of child support collection. If the obligor has any of these benefits, Chapter 9 will tell you how to tap into them for past-due child support.

Subpoena the employer to send you a copy of the front and back of the last paycheck that the obligor cashed. The back of the paycheck may reveal the bank where the obligor has his checking account and may also reveal his account number. Once you are in receipt of the banking information, you will be able to garnish the obligor's checking account for past-due support money. Previous employers are good for this information as well.

While you are at it, subpoena the bank for other accounts that it may be holding for the obligor. Usually a savings account or

Certificate of Deposit (CD) will be kept with the same bank that holds one's checking account. If you find other accounts, they can be garnished as well.

If employers, or former employers, do not have any information to supply to you, try the trade union to which the obligor belongs. Trade unions should be able to supply "earned income" information as well as information on any benefits, bonuses, commissions, and union benefits received by the obligor.

- If the obligor is the owner of a business that requires a license that costs a lot of money to get—a liquor license, for example—file a judgment lien against it. Without a license, the restaurant or bar that the obligor operates cannot serve liquor, which can be damaging to a business of that sort. In a case like this, the license itself will most likely mean nothing to you. Most of the time, licenses cannot be sold, so you will not be able to convert it into money that way. However, if the obligor's business can go down the tubes without the license, he may be inclined to pay you the past-due child support to regain the usage of the license that now belongs to you. Who knows, you may be able to find a way to have the license legally sold after all. The worst-case scenario would be that the obligor doesn't pay you one dime in past-due child support and you don't relinquish the control over the liquor license. Your position hasn't changed any because you weren't getting any support anyway, but the obligor's business will be damaged in some way, if not completely. It's not a bad deal since you still have other tactics to use.

- If you find any credit card accounts, loans, or any other means of credit listed on the obligor's credit report, subpoena the original application that the obligor completed from the creditor or lender. It may contain information on other assets that are not listed on the credit report. These may be assets that you can garnish or otherwise convert into income.

• If you are able to locate a CD owned by the obligor, you could either garnish the interest that the CD earns or, through a Writ of Execution, you can have the deposit turned over to you. Figure out what will bring you the greatest return before you make your decision.

• If you know the obligor to be a stockholder for publicly traded stock, you will need to subpoena information regarding his stock portfolio from his stock brokerage. It helps if you know who the brokerage is. If not, you will have to find out through one of your sleuthing techniques or go through a government attorney to have a 1099 search done. See Chapter 9 for more information. The government attorney will be able to use federal records to access the obligor's 1099 information (interest earned from banks or other financial institutions). The attorney will be able to find out where the earned interest has come from and what company is holding the money. This information will be reported back to you and you can then subpoena the broker for details on the stock that the obligor owns. A government attorney is the only person who can access 1099 information.

• Chapter 9 tells you how to seize personal property belonging to the obligor. This property can be sold and the profit applied to back child support. Follow the methods outlined when you find property on the credit report or through any of your other means.

• If the obligor owns or at some time owned an aircraft or boat, check to see if it is still registered in his name. If it is, you have hit the jackpot—move to seize and sell it immediately. Aircraft registrations are listed with both the Federal Aviation Administration (call 405-954-3011), and with the state. A boat will be listed with the state, unless its size and tonnage (weight) are such that it must be listed with the federal government as well. To find out, call the state Marine Board and the U.S. Coast Guard.

• Those obligors who are in the military, and other federal employees from whom it may be difficult to collect, can have their incomes garnished. See the chapters that focus exclusively on this.

• If the obligor receives income from a trust fund, subpoena information about the fund from the trustee. Once you know what income the obligor receives from the fund, you can either place a wage withholding on the income or have the income garnished.

other ways to locate assets

• If you believe that the obligor will be receiving an inheritance through someone's will, contact the government office that handles wills in the county where it will eventually be probated and ask for a copy. If he is listed as a beneficiary, have a lien placed on any money due to the obligor.

If an immediate family member of the obligor dies without a will, and you believe that the obligor may receive some inheritance, you may be able to place a lien on the obligor's share of the estate. For this you will need to contact an attorney.

• A percentage of unemployment benefits can be withheld for child support payments. Subpoena information from the obligor's previous employer to find out when the obligor lost his job and any other details that may be important for you to know. Then contact the unemployment office to find out what information it needs from you to begin withholding some of the benefits that the obligor receives. Some states will not allow an *obligee* or private attorney to have unemployment benefits withheld. If the state in which the obligor lives will not allow you to withhold wages, you must work through the state child support agency. Government attorneys are given more leeway in this area and will be able to get a withholding in any state.

• Workers' compensation benefits can also be withheld for child support. If the obligor's employer will not tell you who its insurance carrier is, subpoena for the information. Contact the carrier to request the address it is using to send checks to the obligor, the amount of the payment, and when the benefits will run out. Of course, you will need to provide information to get your process started. Ask about this in your first conversation.

• If the obligor is disabled in some way, you and/or your child may be entitled to disability payments. Pay a visit to the Social Security Administration Office in your area to find out. If you need to know whether the obligor is receiving Social Security benefits, you will have to go through a government attorney.

• If the obligor has received, or is due to receive, a settlement from a lawsuit, you can have this income garnished. Visit the county courthouse in the area where the suit was filed and obtain the names of the attorneys who are representing both the obligor and the person or entity that he is suing. File a Writ of Garnishment against the funds that the obligor is due to receive. If the state in which the obligor lives will not allow you to do this, although most of them will, keep close tabs on the lawsuit and file your garnishment immediately following the settlement. Do not let the obligor know what you are doing. If you do, he will probably try to hide the money as quickly as it comes in.

• If you cannot find any assets that belong to the obligor and you become really desperate, you can search the obligor's trash for anything that might lead to asset information. Look for credit card receipts, bank deposit slips, statements, etc. Legally, once trash is put out on the curb it is public property, so don't worry—you won't be breaking any laws.

- You can also become a phony survey person. Before I got my job as a bill collector for the bank, I worked as a marketing research surveyor. I would call people at their homes to ask their opinions on a variety of topics. I have handled everything from political surveys to surveys about the newest brand of peanut butter. At the end of every survey that I was able to get completed before the consumer hung up on me, I was instructed to ask some personal questions. These questions included what they did for a living, their address, where they banked, and then, of course, would they like to receive a coupon for a free jar of peanut butter (or whatever else was being offered). The surveys that I was assigned to were almost always successful if the consumer knew that he was going to get something at the end.

Search your mind for something that you think the obligor would like to have and that he would be willing to disclose certain information to get. Most people like free things. Just be certain that you make the survey sound believable. Once you have an idea of your "offering," decide what information you need to get from the obligor. Your list might include: where do you bank, what is your occupation, are you married, do you hold MasterCard/Visa accounts, what is your approximate income, etc. Then get to work and put together your "survey." It might go something like this:

Survey person:	Hello, may I speak with Mr. John Doe?
Obligor:	This is John Doe.

Survey person: Mr. Doe, this is Mary Jackson from MMM Marketing in the Ohio Theatre Group and we would like to give you four free front row center tickets to our next production of *Les Miserables*, just for answering a few questions.

Obligor: OK.

Survey person: When did you last visit the theater?

Obligor: Oh, about six months ago.

Survey person: How often do you attend the theater?

Obligor: About two or three times a year.

Survey person: When you purchase tickets for the theater, do you pay for them on a MasterCard or Visa account? By answering this question please know that we will not place you on a mailing list of any type.

Obligor: I usually pay by MasterCard.

Survey person: And which bank is that under?

Obligor: People's Bank of North America.

Survey person: Do you bank with People's as well?

Obligor: Yes.

Survey person: About how many theater shows have you seen in your lifetime?

Obligor: I don't know, maybe fifteen.

Survey person: If you have children, do you take them with you to theater shows?

Obligor: No, I don't take them.

Survey person: Just a few more questions and then we are done. What is your approximate age? Under thirty or over thirty?

Obligor: Over thirty.

Survey person: What is your occupation?

Obligor: I'm a licensed plumber.

Survey person: And your income, is it over or under $50,000?

Obligor: Over $50,000.

Survey person: Thank you for your time, Mr. Doe. You will receive a letter in the mail from the Ohio Theatre Group within fourteen days. The letter will include a number for you to call to claim your free tickets and reserve seats for the show. Have a great day!

Obligor: Thank you.

Of course, you will want to customize your queries to the obligor with a survey that makes sense to you. It's better if you ask someone else to make the call for you so that there's no chance that the obligor will recognize your voice. Also, be sure not to use the names of companies that actually exist. Use your imagination and create names that sound real. The obligor will never know the difference. The key is in the presentation. Sound confident and sincere.

chapter 9

enforcing your child support order

Statistics reveal that only 25 percent of the custodial parents who have child support orders ever receive their money. Therefore, 75 percent of the child support orders entered aren't worth the paper they are printed on. Having a child support order means nothing, unless you get paid. Let's recount what you have learned so far: you have learned how to establish paternity and what to do if you are underage. You have learned how to get a child support order and how to have your order modified if your circumstances have changed. You can find your deadbeat if he skips town and you are able to effectively hire a private attorney and maybe even get legal services for free. You now also know what is legally considered to be income—it's not just what one gets paid in his or her paycheck. Now, one way or the other, you will learn the steps that you can take yourself to get blood from an unyielding stone. Ready? One, two, three, SQUEEZE!

Truth be told, there are many options that you have to get your money. The problem is that most people don't know about them. The officials who are paid to help you either don't know about these options or they don't want to tell you because most likely it will create more work. By now you have noticed that this book is about work. How much work are you willing to do to collect your money? Just how mad are you? Are you not going to take it anymore? If you are willing to do the work, then you will get your money.

Most people know about wage withholding. That's when they take the money that is due to you directly from the obligor's paycheck. That's not all there is, but we will begin there because it is the simplest way to get what you want.

wage withholding

A wage withholding (also called an order withholding earnings or a payroll deduction) is a court order requiring the obligor's employer to deduct money from his paycheck and forward it to you or to the state agency. It is the easiest way to collect your money and it has a lot of benefits.

• Once notified and presented with a court order, the employer cannot refuse to deduct and forward the money.

• The employer must forward the money no later than ten days after the deduction.

• If the obligor quits or is fired, the employer is required to inform you, and tell you where the new job is if they know.

• Under federal law, a wage withholding must be permitted for anyone who has a child support order where the payments are thirty days past due or if three consecutive payments have been missed. So as long as the obligor keeps his job, you will have a steady payment coming to you. Keep in mind that typically you can only get about 60 percent of the paycheck amount plus an additional 5 percent for *arrearages* over twelve weeks if the obligor has not remarried and has no dependents. If the obligor has remarried and has dependents, the amount that can be deducted decreases to 50 percent and 5 percent for arrearages over twelve weeks.

You can get a wage withholding through your local child support agency or by going to court yourself and filing an order to withhold earnings. Take a look at Item #5, the Ex Parte Order to Withhold Earnings. This is the motion you will use when you file for wage withholding, so take a few moments to familiarize yourself with it.

Simply get the form from an office supply store, fill it out, and submit it to the court clerk. The small fee involved will probably be about $5.

wage garnishment

Many people confuse wage withholdings with wage garnishments. They use the two terms interchangeably, as though they mean the same thing. Be aware: they don't have the same meaning nor do they work the same way. While a wage withholding is an order from the court to deduct a certain amount of money on a continuous basis and send it to you regularly; a wage garnishment is an order from the court to deduct one lump sum of money (usually a large sum) and send it to you. A wage garnishment is a one-time deal. You will not get regular payments and it does not permit for future child support that may become due. It does have its benefits, however. How would you like to go to court for past-due child support, get awarded a judgment for the amount past due, and then have that entire amount taken out of the obligor's check at once! It can be done. Just thinking of it gives me goose bumps. Remember that the only way you could lose your court case is if the money is not owed to you. If you have a court order in place, and the obligor is in arrears, the only defense he has is mistaken identity. If he does not show up in court, you automatically win.

interstate wage withholding

If your obligor lives in another state, you can still get an *interstate wage withholding*. Simply visit the child support office in your area and they will handle the whole thing for you. If you are pursuing the case on your own, it's not much different than handling a case that's in-state. Prepare the forms and bring them to the family court in your county and give them to the clerk. You will then have to arrange to have the order served to the employer. If you have an obligor on your hands who is a real pain in the neck, prepare yourself to bulldoze him. This goes for the interstate obligors as well as the obligor who lives in-state. Reread Chapter 8 and withhold earnings or garnish anything and everything that the obligor receives as income. We are not just talking about paychecks here. The plan is to make his life so miserable that it would be easier to pay you than to have his funds constantly intercepted.

writ of garnishment (personal property)

Paychecks are not the only things that can be garnished. Any liquid property (cash) that the obligor owns can be garnished for child support. This includes savings and checking accounts, CDs, etc.

Personal property that is not money, but can be seized and sold for money, can also be garnished. In the event that you have found the obligor's liquid assets (cash) and you would like to seize them (take them away), you will need to file a Writ of Garnishment. A Writ of Garnishment is filed with a banking institution, employer, or some other third party that is holding money for the obligor. This is different from a wage garnishment because a wage garnishment takes money directly and only from earnings. A Writ of Garnishment takes money from a source where the money is just sitting. Some examples might be bank accounts, IRAs, etc. If your obligor has taken his liquid property (cash) from one of these sources and transferred it to a friend or relative to prevent you from getting your hands on it, you must obtain it in another way. In this instance, you must file what is called a *creditor's bill*. We will discuss how creditor's bills work later in the chapter.

A Writ of Garnishment is an order from the court demanding that the third party that is holding money for the obligor turn it over to the court. Similar to the wage garnishment, it is a one-time lump sum that does not provide for future child support, but it can pay you what's past due. If you have a child support order and the obligor owes you $3,000 in past-due support and you find an account with $3,500 in it, you can have the account "garnished" for $3,000. If the account you find has only $800, you can wipe out the $800 and the obligor will still owe the remaining $2,200.

When you have located the funds in the bank or other banking institution, call them and ask what their specific procedures are for garnishing an account. Most institutions have several branches and you will need to know which branch needs to be served with your writ. Then go to your office supply store and get a bank garnishment form. Complete the form and take it to the court clerk with whatever small fee is required and file the paperwork. You will also need to arrange to have the paperwork served. See Item #6, Writ of Garnishment.

Writs must be answered in five days. Generally, you will not have a problem with a banking institution since they are accustomed to receiving documents of this type. Once the court receives the money, it is required to hold it for approximately ten days before releasing it to you. This gives anyone who denies owing the money a chance to request a hearing. Common objections are that the money belongs to someone other than the obligor or that the money is exempt from garnishment.

If the obligor states that the money belongs to someone other than himself, he must be able to prove this. If he says that a portion of the funds is exempt, and can prove it, you will receive the remaining balance. An example of exemption would be: in most states you are only permitted to take a percentage of the obligor's paycheck during a garnishment—usually 25 percent. If the obligor can prove that the entire $3,000 that was taken from his bank account consisted of deposited paychecks, then you would be entitled to 25 percent of each paycheck. If the obligor deposited three weekly paychecks of $1,000 per week, you would get $750 and the rest would be returned. In the meantime, however, you would have certainly ticked him off and maybe shaken him up enough to decide to pay up and not to mess with your child support anymore. In addition, if this were a checking account from which the money was taken, checks would be bouncing all over town. If the money was obtained from a CD or stock that had to be sold, the interest would be lost and perhaps there would be penalties to pay. Now, doesn't that make you smile?

writ of garnishment (personal property in the hands of a third party)

Personal property in the hands of a third party can be garnished as well. The only drawback is that most people don't understand it. Banks are used to getting garnishments that they must fulfill, the neighborhood mechanic is not. For example, the fancy car that you want to garnish is at the dealership for its scheduled and predictable 40,000-mile checkup. You have the Writ of Garnishment served to the dealership and they have no choice but to hand the car over. In this instance, they would have to notify the sheriff's department that the car is in their possession. The sheriff would come and remove the vehicle and place it in storage in the same manner as if it was taken from the obligor's home. The same procedures would then follow.

If you find yourself serving a garnishment to a mechanic or other entity that may not be accustomed to garnishment procedures, be sure to contact them (the owner or manager) and make them aware of their responsibility. Otherwise, an unknowing employee may release the vehicle and you will have to start from scratch.

writ of execution (personal property)

Personal property that is in the hands of the obligor can also be taken away. It can then be sold and the profit turned over to you. This process is a bit more complicated and will cost you more to do, but the benefits can be great! Close your eyes for a moment and imagine the obligor leaving his workplace at the end of the day only to find that his car is gone. Better yet, he awakens early on a Saturday morning to a knock at the door. He opens the door and sees the sheriff standing there with an order in his hands to seize his household belongings. It can happen. But don't get your hopes up yet, the procedures that you must follow are enough to cause anyone to turn and walk away. So I ask you—how badly do you want your money?

A Writ of Execution first begins at your family clerk court office. There you will ask the clerk to file a Writ of Execution, which will cost you about $5. Item # 7 is a Writ of Execution. You will see that it instructs the sheriff to seize the property. The Writ of Execution must be issued to the sheriff along with Item # 8, which is a Sheriff's Instruction. A Sheriff's Instruction tells the sheriff what items must be seized. You must provide the sheriff with specific details of the item or items on the list. If you are seizing a car, for example, you must include the year, make, model, color, vehicle identification number, and some type of proof that the car belongs to the obligor. You must also tell the sheriff where the property will be located and when it will be there. The sheriff will charge you a fee for seizing the property—usually about $50. You will also be required to post a bond in the event that the sheriff is sued for seizing property that should not have been taken. The amount of the bond will be based on the value of the property that is being seized. The sheriff may ask you to approximate the value of the property. If you are seizing a car, or any other personal property, and you estimate the value to be $10,000, you can expect to pay anywhere from $100 to $300 for the bond. As a rule of thumb, the bond will cost 1 to 3 percent of the total estimated value of the property. You can get a bond by contacting a bondsman, insurance agent, or attorney. You will also be required to pay for a tow truck or a moving van for the items being removed. The sheriff will take the seized personal belongings to a storage facility, where they will stay, until the sheriff holds a "sheriff's sale" and the items are sold. You must also pay the storage fee. All of these fees must be paid up front before any seizure of personal property can take place. This is why you must be committed to a "by any means necessary" policy to get your child support. You can see why many people do not go this route. Sure, you can add the fees that you had to pay out onto the judgment that the obligor owes to you, but if you are like most custodial parents, you don't have the money to do this.

There are some items that the government will not permit you to take from the obligor, because they may be essential to his basic living. A car or any furniture is exempt up to the value of $1,500. Books and tools are exempt up to $750, and a rifle up to $500. If the personal property you wish to seize is worth a lot of money, much more than would be required to satisfy your judgment and the additional fees entailed, including the cost of the sale, then you may consider enlisting help from someone in the form of a temporary loan. Keep in mind that you can only get the amount of money that the property sells for, minus the cost of the sale. If the car valued at $10,000 sells for $4,000 at the auction and the cost of the sale was $200, you will receive $3,800, less the exemption of $1,500. If you invested $1,000 to have the property seized, you net $1,300.

So before you decide to seize personal property and have it sold to pay your past-due child support, check your numbers and make sure that you don't get caught behind the eight ball. Food for thought: you could always have the personal property seized and sold and willingly break even just for the fun of it.

You could also bid on the property yourself—up to the amount of your judgment—and own the property without any out-of-pocket costs. You can do this because you have a judgment for the amount of your unpaid child support, and you have a judgment lien on the property, so you will receive the proceeds of the sale, up to the amount of your judgment. If the bidding goes higher than the amount of your judgment, pay a little extra, if you can afford it. If the property is yours, you can then sell it privately for more money if it is worth it, or you can keep it.

writ of execution (real property)

Writs of Execution can also be filed against real property (real estate) to prevent someone from selling property without paying you first, or to force a foreclosure in order to get your past-due child support. A Writ of Execution against real property is more complex than a Writ of Execution against personal property. In this circumstance, it is best that you seek help from an attorney, if you can. Before you do, use your investigative techniques learned in Chapter 7 to discover the value of the house and how much equity the obligor has in it. Equity is the amount of money that has been invested in the property. For example, if a house was purchased for $100,000 and $50,000 has been paid between the down payment and mortgage payments, there is $50,000 of equity in the house (remember that a portion of every mortgage payment goes to interest). Since you will need to pay out a lot of fees to force the sale, and there are costs associated with the sale, you will need to know how much you can get out of the house before you proceed. Again, you need to keep yourself from getting caught behind the eight ball. The amount of money that is exempt will be between $12,000 and $15,000. Also confirm that his name is listed on the deed because you will need to prove that the house belongs to the obligor. In some states, a home cannot be foreclosed on at all because of the Homestead Act. Your trusty attorney should be able to tell you if your obligor is in one of those states.

Sounds like a headache, doesn't it? There is good news, however. When threatened with a foreclosure due to a judgment on their property, most people will find a way to pay the judgment rather than take the chance of losing their property. It's a game of "uncle." Sometimes just showing him that you mean business will get you what you want.

creditor's bill

There are countless cases where the obligor will go to any length to avoid paying child support. Obligors will lie about their assets and income. They will place assets into a corporate name to avoid ownership. They have also been known to transfer assets into someone else's name, usually a new spouse or significant other. In this case, you will need to file a motion that is called a creditor's bill. A creditor's bill is simply a lawsuit that you are filing against the person who is in possession of the property that you believe was transferred. Transferring property to avoid paying child support is illegal. By filing a lawsuit against the person holding the property, you will be able to subject him to the scrutiny of subpoenas and interrogatories to discover how he obtained the property. Once you are able to prove that the property used to belong to the obligor, you will be able to get a judgment lien on the property and proceed with a sheriff seizure or foreclosure. Again, check your numbers to make sure that it's worth it. One word of caution: this is another one of those complicated cases where you may need to enlist the help of an attorney. At least you know what you need, and you know what to ask for.

till-tap

This is one of my personal favorites. If your obligor owns a store that is open to the public and that has a cash register, wait until the busiest time of year and file a Sheriff's Instruction for a till-tap. During a till-tap, the sheriff will go to the obligor's place of business and empty out the cash register—lock, stock, and barrel. Since you will want to get all the cash that you possibly can, you will want to instruct the sheriff to go after the busiest time of day. Hopefully there will still be some customers in the store to witness this action. If you don't know when the busiest time of the year or of the day is, do some research and find out. Call stores similar to the one that your obligor owns and tell them that you are doing some research—most people would be happy to answer a few short questions. Better yet, have someone your obligor doesn't know call his store and get the exact information you need.

credit report investigations

I know an obligor who left his wife and children and soon thereafter took up with another woman. He paid no child support to his family, though he was very wealthy. For five years, his first wife tried to track him down as he moved from state to state to avoid paying her. He placed money in overseas accounts and property in his new wife's name. They later adopted children and moved into a mansion. Because she was relentless, his first wife eventually caught up with him and he was jailed. There are obligors who will fight tooth and nail to avoid paying child support. This man was obviously one of them. What disturbs me is that state agencies aided him and his new wife with the lifestyle that they led. If child support arrearages were noted on this man's credit report, he never would have been able to adopt the children that he and his wife had. This is one of the reasons that I am a staunch supporter of reporting past-due child support to the credit agencies. It happens frequently. Obligors go on to live lavish lifestyles while leaving their children in the lurch. They purchase homes, new cars, take vacations, and adopt children. If past-due support was listed on credit reports, they would not be able to accomplish such feats until the support was paid. If your obligor owes you six months or more of past-due child support, simply contact your local agency and insist that they do this.

payment guarantee

In some states, the court may require that the obligor post a bond, or a cash payment, to assure future child support. If the obligor fails to make a scheduled payment, the payment is taken from the bond, or cash payment, and forwarded to the custodial parent. In New York, when you file your court documents requesting a hearing for this matter, cite 471 Family Court Act. In North Carolina, you must show that the obligor showed "intentional disregard for the financial obligation to the family." In other words, you must show that the obligor spent inordinate amounts of money on unnecessary goods. Instead of a bond or a cash payment, it is called a trust fund and it is set up for a period of three years.

If your state does not have a provision for the guarantee of payment, a letter to your congressperson is in order. Write asking that she sponsor an act for the guarantee of child support. See Item #9.

If your congressperson gets enough of these letters, it would be nearly impossible for her to turn a deaf ear to the requests.

EX PARTE ORDER TO WITHHOLD EARNINGS

IN THE CIRCUIT COURT OF THE STATE OF [STATE NAME]
FOR THE COUNTY OF [COUNTY NAME]

[YOUR NAME],	)	No. 0000
Petitioner,	)	
	)	
and	)	EX PARTE ORDER
	)	TO WITHHOLD EARNINGS
[OBLIGOR'S NAME],	)	
Respondent	)	

TO: Employer   [Obligor's Name]
          Address   Social Security Number

Based upon Petitioner's Motion,
YOU ARE   DELINQUENT
HEREBY   AMOUNT OWED $_____
ORDERED TO   CONTINUING MONTHLY
WITHHOLD &   SUPPORT
PAY OVER TO: PAYMENTS: $ _____

An amount equal to 25 percent (or the continuing monthly support payment amount, whichever is less) of the beneficiary's benefits for temporary total disability, or an amount equal to 25 percent of the beneficiary's benefits for permanent partial disability and permanent total disability due or becoming due for each month beneficiary becomes or is eligible for these benefits, whether the benefits are paid monthly or in a lump sum payment.

The Department of Human Resources will inform you when there is no longer a current monthly support obligation.

EVEN IF THERE IS MORE THAN ONE ORDER TO WITHHOLD, IN NO EVENT SHALL YOU WITHHOLD MORE THAN 25 PERCENT OF BENEFICIARY'S BENEFITS DUE OR BECOMING DUE FOR EACH MONTH BENEFICIARY BECOMES OR IS ELIGIBLE.

THIS ORDER supersedes any order to withhold previously entered and shall continue in effect as long as there is current support owed or until further order of this court.

DATED _____   _____
                                CIRCUIT COURT JUDGE

WRIT OF GARNISHMENT

IN THE _____ COURT OF THE STATE OF [STATE NAME]

For the county of _____.

_____.

_____Plaintiff

Case No. _____
Writ of Garnishment

_____

_____ Defendant(s)

IN THE NAME OF THE STATE OF [STATE NAME], TO:

_____

You are now a garnishee.

AS A GARNISHEE, YOU NEED TO KNOW THE FOLLOWING (the following information is to be filled in by the creditor):

On [DATE], plaintiff/defendant(cross out one)_____, named above and called "Creditor", has obtained a judgment (a court order for the payment of money) against the plaintiff/defendant (cross out one) _____, named above and called "Debtor." The Debtor's Social Security Number or employee identification number is _____ (insert if known).

The following amount is necessary to satisfy the Creditor's judgment:

+Judgment debt	$_____	_____	$_____
+Prejudgment interest	$_____	_____	$_____
+Attorney Fees	$_____	Total other from additional sheet	
+Cost Bill	$_____	(if used)	$_____
+Post-Judgment Interest	$_____	+ Past Writ Issuance Fees	$_____
+Delivery Fee for this Writ	$_____	+ Past Delivery Fees	$_____
+Sheriff Fees other than		+ Transcript and Filing Fees	
Delivery Fees	$_____	for other counties	$_____
+Other (Explain. Attach additional		= Subtotal	$_____
sheets if necessary.)	$_____	LESS Payments Made	($_____)
_____	$_____	= TOTAL Amounts Required to Satisfy	
_____	$_____	in Full this Judgment	$_____

THE CLERK OF THE COURT HAS NOT CALCULATED ANY AMOUNTS ON THE WRIT AND IS NOT LIABLE FOR ERRORS MADE IN THE WRIT BY THE CREDITOR.

Item #6: Writ of Garnishment

I certify that I have read the Writ of Garnishment; and to the best of my knowledge, information, and belief, there is good ground to support it.

DATED _____, 20_____

Signature of Creditor's Attorney _____

Type or Print Creditor's Attorney _____

Address _____ Date _____

WRIT OF EXECUTION

In the _____ Court of the State of [State Name]

For the County of [County Name]

_____ No. _____

_____.

Plaintiff

Vs.   **EXECUTION**

_____.

_____.

Defendant

To _____ County, Any State

WHEREAS ON _____ in the _____ Court of _____County, Any State, _____

Recovered a judgment from _____

_____ for the following sum(s):

Which judgment, or a certified transcript thereof, was on [Date], duly docketed in the judgment docket of the _____ Court of [County Name], [State Name], where it remains in force and unsatisfied in whole or in part;

THEREFORE, IN THE NAME OF THE STATE OF [STATE NAME], you are commanded that out of the personal property of the said judgment debtor(s), or if sufficient personal property cannot be found, then out of the real property belonging to said judgment debtor(s) on or after the date said judgment was docketed in your county, excepting such as the law exempts, that you satisfy the amount of said judgment with interest and costs and disbursements that may have accrued, LESS the amount of $_____ which has been paid on said judgment, and also the costs of this writ, and make due return of this writ within sixty days after you receive this writ.

Witness my hand and the seal of this court on this _____ day of _____, 20_____

Judgment Debt	$_____	
Interest	$_____	_____
Attorney Fee	$_____	Name and Title
Cost Bill	$_____	By _____
Deputy		
Additional Costs	$_____	
Total	$_____	
Payments Made	$_____	Issued at the request of:
Balance Due	$_____	
Accruing Costs	$_____	
Disbursements	$_____	_____
Keeper's Fees	$_____	_____
Mileage	$_____	_____
Total	$_____	_____

Item #7: Writ of Execution   121

SHERIFF'S INSTRUCTION

IN THE CIRCUIT COURT OF THE STATE OF [STATE NAME]
FOR THE COUNTY OF [COUNTY NAME]

In the matter of:	)	
[YOUR NAME],	)	No. 1111
	)	
Petitioner	)	
	)	INSTRUCTIONS TO
and	)	SHERIFF
	)	
	)	[(County Name)]
[OBLIGOR'S NAME],	)	
	)	
Respondent	)	

TO THE SHERIFF OF [COUNTY NAME]:

YOU ARE HEREBY INSTRUCTED to execute the enclosed Writ of Execution for the following described personal property of the defendant, to-wit:

[INSERT DESCRIPTION OF PERSONAL PROPERTY]

by immediately proceeding to debtor's residence located at [Obligor's Street Address, City, and State], or to such other location as may be hereafter identified within your county and at such place or places to then and there take possession of the equipment described above from the respondent or his agents or employees or any other person who may be in possession thereof and deliver it to the petitioner.

Enclosed is our check in the amount of $50 as a deposit to cover your fees and expenses. If you have any questions or problems, please contact the undersigned. Thank you for your assistance.

> [Your name or your attorney's name
> Street address
> Town, State, Zip Code
> Telephone Number with Area Code]

[Date
Your name
Your street address
City, State, Zip Code]

[Congressperson
Street address
City, State, Zip Code]

Dear [Congressperson's Name],

I am writing to request that you sponsor an act for the guarantee of child support in [Your State Name]. New York and North Carolina have such laws. If the obligor repeatedly misses child support payments he/she may be required to post a surety bond or advance cash payment to provide for future child support payments in the event that they fall behind. If [Your State Name] had such a law, it would aid in preventing my child support from lagging so far behind.

Please respond to this letter.

Sincerely,

[Your name]

what the courts can do for you

a s you are working to get your child support, you will find that there are many people who will not be helpful to you. It may happen for a variety of reasons—sometimes it will simply be because they are ignorant and don't know how to help you. They may not know how to obtain the information that you are requesting to give it to you. It's easier to be rude to you than to admit that they don't have the slightest idea of what you are asking. Depending on what source you go to and to whom you speak, they may be actively trying to protect the absent parent. And sometimes, it will be a combination of inep-titude and sheer meanness. Whatever the case, you don't have to feel as though you must beg for the information that you seek. If you have a legal and valid reason for digging into the personal financial life of someone, the law allows you to do it.

subpoena

Let's say that you are certain that the obligor has accounts with an investment company, but you don't have any account numbers or any other means of proof. You call and/or write to the company and ask that they release the information to you on the basis that you have a judgment against their client. Not surprisingly, they refuse any information to you. If this happens to you, take comfort in the fact that you can subpoena any information that you wish to know from them, as long as your petition has been filed with the court and you have been given a case number. You can find out how many accounts the obligor has, how much money is in them, when they were opened, as well as any personal information that they may have on the obligor. They may have a current address, employment information, and other bank account or credit information, and it is all available to you through a subpoena.

A subpoena is a court order that demands that the entity being subpoenaed (the investment company, in this case) appear as a witness to answer questions. In this case, you would want to ask questions about the obligor's finances and other personal information that they may have. If you want them to bring supporting documentation (statements, deposit slips, etc.), you must file a subpoena *duces tecum*. This requires that they not only appear, but that they bring whatever paperwork you want them to bring. In most cases, you will only need to file subpoenas as a scare tactic. Once served with a subpoena, the most uncooperative person will suddenly provide you with what you need rather than take the time to appear and answer your questions. Simply make contact after the subpoena has been properly served and ask if they would prefer to provide the information that you request or if they would rather appear in person. Nine times out of ten, they will comply if it will get them off the hook. Remember to have them send to you copies of all of the supporting documents. Use the subpoena liberally. It can provide a wealth of information.

If your obligor has moved out of town without leaving a trace, and you are certain that someone in his family must know where he is, though no one will say a word, you can subpoena them all to give you whatever information you need. A subpoena is issued under penalty of law, so they must comply or face the judge themselves. It's also a good way to get information from someone who would like to spill the beans but fears some type of reprisal. If subpoenaed, he would have no other choice but to talk. A subpoena can be a beautiful thing. Re-read Chapter 8 and consider the possibilities.

To obtain a subpoena form, contact your court clerk. Some courts require it to be stamped or certified by the court, and you may have to pay a small fee. You must have a court case to use a subpoena, and you must put your case number on the subpeona.

If the court clerk does not have a subpoena form, you can get one from your local office supply store. After filling out the form, take it to the clerk's office to be signed. You may have to pay a small fee for this service (approximately $5). You must then have someone other than yourself, who is over the age of eighteen, serve (deliver) the subpoena upon your witness. The only catch is that it must be personally delivered. It cannot be mailed or given to a secretary, co-worker, neighbor, etc. In addition, you must pay the witness for attending court and the travel involved. You can expect to pay no more than $25 for an appearance and 10 cents per mile for travel. After the clerk signs the subpoena, you will need to make two copies of it. Keep one of the copies for yourself. The other copy and the original will need to be given to your "process server" (the person you select to serve the subpoena) to serve to your witness along with the fees for the appearance and mileage. Keep in mind that a witness may only be legally required to make an appearance to answer your subpoena if it is in the same county in which he lives, works, or conducts business. Most people would be hesitant to snub a subpoena. If you can't get to the county in which he lives or works, have the subpoena served anyway. The witness may not know that he doesn't have to appear.

If your witness would rather end up in a legal proceeding than deal with you directly, you will need to provide a place for the *deposition* to take place. A deposition is the legal term for the question and answer period that will take place between you and your witness. A deposition can take place at almost any location. It does not have to be at a court building. If you do wish to have it at the courthouse, you will have to arrange with the clerk to have a private room. Otherwise, it can take place at your home or office, the witness' home or office, or anywhere else you desire. You will need to provide a court reporter. A court reporter is someone who will record the questions and answers during the deposition. Expect to pay $30 to $55 an hour for a court reporter. You can get a *transcript* (written record) of the deposition for an additional fee. Be sure to ask what the fee is before you request one. By the end of your deposition you will have all the information that your witness can provide to you.

judgment debtor exam

Sometimes the only person who can provide the information that you need is the obligor himself. If that is the case, you will need to file a judgment debtor exam. A judgment debtor exam is similar to a subpoena in that the court is requiring someone to appear and answer questions. The difference between the two is that the subpoena is served upon any person, other than the obligor, whom you would like to call as a witness, to come and answer questions about the obligor. A judgment debtor exam is served upon the obligor to answer questions about his personal financials or whatever else may be necessary. The most difficult task when planning a judgment debtor exam can be finding the obligor in order to have him served. In some cases, you know where he is and you suspect or know that he has cash or assets, you just can't get to them. If you don't know where the obligor is, or if he tends to be a bit elusive and only comes out at night like a vampire, then it makes your job more difficult. If your obligor is vampire-like, then you will need to re-read Chapter 7 and find more methods to flush him out. If you know where he is and he is doing a good job of hiding what he has, read on.

The first thing you should know is that rarely will a judge allow you to conduct a debtor exam until you have first attempted to execute on personal or real property, and failed, or until you have sent a Notice of Demand to Pay Judgment (Item #11) and it has been ignored. My personal strategy would be to send the demand letter first. Most deadbeats ignore demand letters, especially when they are from someone to whom they owe child support. He will laugh it off and muse at the humor of it all. That's exactly what you want him to do. Of course, you also want your money, and if after receiving your demand letter your obligor pays you, then you have what you want, right? Right. But what you don't have is the abundance of knowledge that a judgment debtor exam can provide to you. During a debtor exam you can ask the obligor about cash he may have on hand, in an account, or invested. You may ask if anyone is holding any cash for him in any form. You may ask about any personal or real property that he may own or have transferred recently. In short, you can find out the value of everything that he has. This serves two purposes for you: first, you can begin to form a list of things that you may want to have seized by the sheriff. If you have never been inside of the obligor's home, how else would you know what he has? Second, it will do your soul good to have the deadbeat squirm a bit.

The obligor may lie during the exam, which is why you want to have him bring all of the supporting documents so that you may examine them. This includes, but is not limited to, tax returns, pay stubs, checkbooks, bank statements, etc. You can make the list as long as you like as long as it is relevant. The obligor can also decide not to show up at the exam. If he decides not to show, the judge can order (and you will ask that the judge order) a bench warrant for his arrest.

Chances are that if this is your first time appearing before the judge requesting a bench warrant because the obligor did not appear, the judge is likely instead to order a *show cause* hearing for contempt. This gives the obligor one last chance to appear and answer your questions. If he does not show a second time, a warrant may be issued.

It is important to understand that it is the judge's decision whether or not to order a bench warrant for the arrest of the obligor. There are no hard and fast rules here. A judge may order a warrant for the first failure to appear, or she may order it for the second failure to appear. She may not order it at all and you will have to persist to get one issued. For this reason, you want to be sure that you have all of your facts correct and you present them to the judge in such a way that it is practically impossible for her to turn you down. Explain the hardships that the obligor has put you through in your pursuit to collect child support from him. Outline the many times that the obligor has refused to appear in court or has finagled his way out of a court order somehow. Tell the judge everything and leave out nothing. Read your statement to the judge before asking for the bench warrant for contempt of court.

Once you have been able to sway the judge in your direction and the obligor is subsequently arrested, he will be held until you can get there to conduct your examination, or until he is able to post bail, if the judge sets a bail. The bail amount should be equal to the amount of past-due child support. If the obligor is able to post bail, you can garnish it.

If the obligor lives in another state, or if it would be too difficult for you to travel to conduct a judgment debtor exam, some states will allow you to do it by mail instead. This is called a *written interrogatory*. If you are interested in this method, call the clerk of the court in your county and ask if your state allows this type of debtor exam. You will be able to write down the list of questions that you want your obligor to answer. This list can be either personally delivered to the obligor or delivered by certified mail. The completed interrogatory must be returned to you within twenty days, along with any supporting documentation that you have requested. If it is not, the same procedure as above applies. Remember that each motion that you file will require small fees to be paid at the courthouse, as well as service fees if you hire a process server or the sheriff to serve the obligor. Only plan on conducting a debtor exam or interrogatory if you are dealing with high stakes and would bet your bottom dollar that the obligor is sitting on a gold mine that should belong to you and your children.

To conduct a judgment debtor exam, not only must you serve the obligor, but you must also file a motion with the court to conduct the exam (Item #12). The motion must state where, when, and at what time the obligor must appear in court. (The court clerk will provide you with this information when the judge signs your order—Item #13.) It must advise the obligor that he must answer questions under oath and, if you so desire, it may also provide a restraining order. The restraining order will advise the obligor that he may not sell, transfer, or dispose of any assets before the exam takes place. It may also state the supporting documentation that you are requiring the obligor to bring. During the same visit, you must file an affidavit stating that you either attempted to execute on property belonging to the obligor or that you sent a demand letter and did not receive full or partial payment (Item #14). The judge will then sign the order, and the clerk will give you a certified copy to serve upon the obligor. There are some states that will allow you to serve the obligor by certified letter, but check with the court clerk before doing this.

On the day that you and your obligor must appear in court, the judge will call every debtor who is there to be examined. One by one, like a herd of cattle, they will be sworn in. After your obligor has given his oath you can then proceed to a quiet place (any quiet place will do) to go ahead with your exam. If there are any documents or answers to your questions that need to be clarified, you can go into the courtroom and have the judge make the final determination. During your exam you may discover that the obligor has some non-exempt assets. If you do, go immediately to the judge when your exam is over and request that an order for the obligor to turn over the non-exempt items be issued. Item #15 is an example of some of the questions that you may want to ask your obligor.

contempt of court

The person being charged with contempt of court faces jail time because he has not done what the court has ordered. In your case, if your obligor is being charged with contempt, he has not paid court-ordered child support. Everyone is urged to utilize this method of child support collection, though it is not a cure-all. In fact, it may not work at all. Basically, what contempt of court will do is to drag the obligor into court to explain why he hasn't paid child support. Rarely will a judge order jail time for an obligor for his first contempt of court charge. Usually obligors get far too many chances to pay before a judge will order a warrant for their arrest. If the obligor is arrested, child support must be paid before the obligor is released.

That's where the system gets weak. The obligor should be required to pay all back child support before being released. Anyone who has been through the process can tell you that is not the case. More often than not, the judge releases the obligor with a warning and requires him to pay only a portion of the child support before being released.

Although the contempt of court proceeding leaves much to be desired, there are several reasons for suggesting that you use it.

- If you only get 50 percent of what the obligor owes you, that's 50 percent more than you had before.

- If you have to file repeated motions for contempt of court, eventually the judge will give the obligor jail time.

- If you get nothing else, you will get the satisfaction of seeing that the obligor was jailed.

- I suggest that you employ every method that you can legally, physically, and mentally handle at one time. As the saying goes, if you throw enough mud on the wall, something has to stick.

A contempt of court proceeding is filed the same way any other motion is filed. Visit the clerk's office for the appropriate forms or pick them up at your office supply store. You will need to simultaneously file a motion for an Order to Show Cause and an affidavit (Items #16 and #17). The motion for the Order to Show Cause states that the obligor must appear in court to explain the reasons why he should not be held in contempt for failing to pay child support. The affidavit will outline the reasons why he should be. You should attach a copy of your court order stating the amount of child support that was ordered, as well as a detailed account of missed payments and payments received, if any. These forms will need to be filed with the court clerk, who will tell you when to appear in court. You will receive a certified copy of the Order to Show Cause (Item #18), which must be served upon the obligor. Of course, you will keep a copy for yourself before you hand over the original.

At this point, the case is very clear-cut and, unless the obligor can come up with some proof of payment, he will be held in contempt. The only defense that he may have is that an illness or disability has prevented him from making the payments. Unemployment or underemployment is also often used as a defense, but it holds no legal grounds.

What happens from this point is purely potluck. It depends upon the judge assigned to you, what her personal beliefs are, and maybe her mood that day. The law allows for jail time for an obligor on his first contempt hearing. It allows the obligor to stay in jail until able to come up with the entire amount of back child support that he owes. None of this ever happens, however. Generally, he will be let off on a warning with a small amount of support paid. Unpaid child support will be considered arrearages and will be ordered to be paid off slowly. But holding the contempt hearing is better than not holding it. The threat of jail will continually hang over his head and if you have the kind of obligor who keeps you running back and forth to court on contempt charges, eventually his luck will run out.

SUBPOENA

IN THE CIRCUIT COURT OF THE STATE OF [STATE NAME]
FOR THE COUNTY OF [COUNTY NAME]

[YOUR NAME],	)	
Plaintiff	)	No. 0000
	)	
vs.	)	CIVIL SUBPOENA
	)	DUCES TECUM
[OBLIGOR'S NAME],	)	
Defendant	)	

TO: [Obligor's Name
        Address
        City, State Zip Code]

IN THE NAME OF THE STATE OF [STATE NAME]:

You are hereby required to appear on the _____ day of _____, 20___, commencing at _____A.M./P.M., at the home of [Your Name], Plaintiff, [Your Address], for your deposition by the plaintiff. You are required to appear and remain in attendance until the completion of your deposition. You are further required to bring with you any and all documents which are set forth on Exhibit A attached hereto and by reference incorporated herein.

ISSUED this _____ day of _____, 20____.

NOTICE OF DEMAND TO PAY JUDGMENT

IN THE CIRCUIT COURT OF THE STATE OF [STATE NAME]
FOR THE COUNTY OF [COUNTY NAME]

[YOUR NAME],	)	NO. 0000
Plaintiff	)	
	)	
vs.	)	NOTICE OF DEMAND TO
	)	PAY JUDGMENT
[OBLIGOR'S NAME],	)	
Defendant	)	

TO: [Obligor's Name
Address
City, State Zip Code]
Defendant.

DEMAND IS HEREBY MADE upon you pursuant to State Statutes, for payment, within ten days of your receipt of this Notice, of that certain Judgment entered against you in the above court. Payment may be made through the court or to the undersigned.

PLEASE TAKE NOTICE THAT your failure to pay will result in further court proceedings. **TOTAL AMOUNT DUE: $**_____.
DATED this ___ day of _____, 20____.

_____
Plaintiff

MOTION FOR EXAMINATION OF
JUDGMENT DEBTOR

IN THE CIRCUIT COURT OF [STATE NAME]
FOR THE COUNTY OF [COUNTY NAME]

[YOUR NAME],	)	
Plaintiff	)	No. 0000
	)	
vs.	)	MOTION FOR EXAMINATION
	)	OF JUDGMENT DEBTOR
[OBLIGOR'S NAME],	)	
Defendant	)	

Plaintiff moves for an order:

1. Requiring Defendant [Obligor's Name] to appear at a time and place to be fixed by the court and answer under oath questions concerning any property or interest in property that defendant may have or claim, and then and there to produce the following documents of the defendant:

2. Refraining defendant from selling, transferring, or in any manner disposing of his property liable to execution, pending this proceeding.

3. This motion is based upon ORS 58.111, the records and the files herein, and (choose one) (either) the return service of an unsatisfied execution (or) proof of service on the attached affidavit of a notice of demand to pay the judgment within 10 days (or) proof of service on file herein of notice of demand to pay judgment within 10 days.

_____

Plaintiff

ORDER FOR EXAMINATION OF
JUDGMENT DEBTOR

IN THE CIRCUIT COURT OF [STATE NAME]
FOR THE COUNTY OF [COUNTY NAME]

[YOUR NAME],	)	
Plaintiff,	)	No. 0000
	)	
vs.	)	ORDER FOR
	)	THE EXAMINATION
[OBLIGOR'S NAME],	)	OF JUDGMENT DEBTOR
Defendant	)	

This matter coming on for hearing on plaintiff's motion for examination of judgment debtor, and it appearing from the records and files herein that the judgment in this matter is unsatisfied and (choose one) (either) an execution herein has been returned unsatisfied (or) a notice of demand to pay judgment within 10 days has been served upon defendant in a manner provided by law, it is hereby

ORDERED that [Obligor's Name] appear before the presiding judge of the above-entitled court in Room No. _____ of the Any County Courthouse, Any City, Any State, on the _____ day of _____, 20____ at the hour of _____, A.M./P.M., and answer under oath questions concerning any property or interest in property that defendant may have or claim, and it is further

ORDERED that Defendant be, and hereby is, restrained from selling, transferring, or in any manner disposing of any of his property liable to execution pending this proceeding.

DATED this ____day of _____, 20____.

_____
CIRCUIT COURT JUDGE

Item #13: Order for Examination of Judgment Debtor

AFFIDAVIT IN SUPPORT OF MOTION

IN THE CIRCUIT COURT OF THE STATE OF [STATE NAME]
IN THE COUNTY OF [COUNTY NAME]

[YOUR NAME],	)	
Plaintiff	)	No. 0000
	)	
vs.	)	AFFIDAVIT IN SUPPORT
	)	OF MOTION
[OBLIGOR'S NAME],	)	
Defendant	)	
	)	
STATE OF [STATE NAME]	)	
	)	
County of [County Name]	)	

I, [Your Name], being first duly sworn, depose and say that:

1. I am the Plaintiff.

2. On or about [Date], I caused a notice of demand to pay judgment to be deposited in the U.S. Mail postage prepaid, in a sealed envelope addressed to [Obligor's Name], defendant, at [Obligor's Address, City, State], by certified mail, return receipt requested.

3. The notice of demand was served upon the defendant on [Date], as shown by the face of the receipt attached. **[Attach a copy of the face of the receipt.]**

4. A true copy of the notice of demand is attached hereto, marked "Exhibit A," and by this reference made part hereof.

_____
Plaintiff

SUBSCRIBED AND SWORN to before me this ____day of _____, 20____.

_____
NOTARY PUBLIC FOR STATE
My Commission Expires: _____

Item #14: **Affidavit in Support of Motion**

SAMPLE QUESTIONS FOR AN ORAL DEBTOR'S
EXAMINATION OR WRITTEN INTERROGATORY

DATE: NAME OF COURT REPORTER, IF ANY

1. **Personal Information**
    A. Full Name:
    B. Residence address:
    C. Residence telephone number:
    D. Spouse's name, occupation, and employer:
    E. How many children under the age of 18?

2. **Occupation**
    A. Employer or name of business:
    B. Type of business:
    C. Your occupation:
    D. Business address:
    E. Business telephone number:
    F. Business associates:
    G. Name of employer's bank, address:
    H. Employment history for the past three years:

3. **Income**
    A. Income from occupation or business:
    B. Incomes from all other sources, including
        pensions, disability, unemployment, and other businesses:
    C. Commissions or renewals earned or anticipated:
    D. Pertinent information from state and federal tax returns and other books
        and records brought to the examination:

4. **Interests in Real Property**
    A. Beneficial or fee interest:
    B. Amount of equity in home and who holds mortgage:
    C. Purchaser or seller on contract: With whom, how much is owed?:
    D. Lessor or lessee:
    E. Remainder or contingent interest:
    F. Beneficial use of any use of any real property in the name of
        another, including spouse:
    G. Mortgage or beneficiary under deed of trust:
    H. Any other interest whatever in any property in your state or any other
        state or country:

5. **Securities**
    A. Stock:
        1. If a shareholder in a close corporation, is the debtor an
            officer or director?

Item #15: Sample Questions for a Debtor's Examination   141

2. Who are the other officers, directors, and major shareholders?

3. Any other stock?

4. Any accounts with brokerage houses:

B. Debt:

1. Checks, drafts, or notes payable to the debtor:

2. Bonds, dividends, certificates, certificates of deposit, deposits, or other interest-bearing instruments:

6.   Cash Equivalent

A.   Cash on hand:

B.   Safe deposit boxes:

C.   Bank, savings and loan, and credit union accounts of any kind:

D.   Deposits of money with any other institution or person:

E.   Cash value on insurance policies:

F.   IRS and state tax refunds due or expected:

7.   Choses In Action

A.   Accounts receivable or debts on open account

B.   Liquidated or unliquidated claims of any nature, including in contract and tort:

C.   Claims against insurance companies:

D.   Security interests and other liens or claims:

8.   Other Personal Property

A.   Household goods:

B.   Automobiles, trucks, motorcycles, and other vehicles:

C.   Boat or other vessel: How much is owed on it?

D.   Inventory, tools, machinery, and fixtures:

E.   Farm equipment, animals, or crops:

F.   Jewelry or other valuable property including sculpture, paintings, antiques, stamps, coins, etc.:

G.   Patents, copyrights, trademarks, trade names, royalties, etc.:

H.   Any documents of title, including warehouse receipts, etc.:

I.   Any interest in any other business, partnership, or joint venture:

J.   Real estate listings:

K.   Any licenses or permits from public authorities:

L.   Any other property, tangible or intangible, which might have a potential value:

9.   Trusts, Etc.

A.   Is any property held for you in trust, guardianship, conservatorship, or custodianship?

B.   Are you a trustee, custodian, guardian or conservator?

C.   Are you an heir of anyone who has passed away?

10. **Legal Proceedings**

    A. Do you now have a legal claim against any party or does any party now have a legal claim against you?

    B. Have you been a party to any legal proceeding over the past three years?

        1. If so, have you satisfied any judgment against you?

        2. Has there been a levy against any of your property?

        3. Has any third party satisfied any judgment for you?

        4. Have you collected any judgment?

    C. In the past three years, has the IRS or any state or county agency asserted a claim for unpaid taxes against you?

11. **Other Indebtedness**

    A. Names and addresses of secured creditors and amounts claimed by each:

    B. Names and addresses of unsecured creditors and amounts claimed by each, including tax collectors:

    C. Names and addresses of judgment creditors, amount of each judgment:

    D. Names and addresses of those to whom you have applied for a loan in the past 3 years:

12. **Transfers And Losses**

    A. Transfers of property within the past 2 years to relatives, charities, trusts, or others:

    B. Money deposited in accounts in the name of another over the past 2 years:

    C. Loans repaid over the past 2 years:

    D. Assignments of payments, notes, contracts, insurance policies, or wages over the past 2 years (Example: purchases of property, including stock, for another over the past 2 years):

    E. Transfers of any property over the past 2 years, not in the usual course of business:

    F. Does anyone else hold title to or possession of any property in which you have any rights or interests?

13. **Books And Records**

    A. Name and address of accountant-bookkeeper:

MOTION AND AFFIDAVIT FOR ORDER
TO SHOW CAUSE, RE: CONTEMPT

IN THE CIRCUIT COURT OF THE STATE OF [STATE NAME]
FOR THE COUNTY OF [COUNTY NAME]

In the Matter of:	)	
	)	No. 0000
[YOUR NAME],	)	
Petitioner	)	
	)	MOTION AND AFFIDAVIT
	)	FOR ORDER TO SHOW
and	)	CAUSE, RE: CONTEMPT
[OBLIGOR'S NAME]	)	
Respondent	)	

Petitioner moves for an order requiring the respondent to appear and show cause, if any there be, why petitioner should not be held in contempt of court for failing to comply with the provisions of the Judgment previously entered herein on or about [Date], as specifically alleged in the affidavit set forth herein below.

Petitioner declares that:

1. The maximum sanction the Petitioner seeks is an order incarcerating respondent in the county jail until he complies with the order of the court by paying child support to the Petitioner.

2. Petitioner seeks a sanction of confinement.

3. Petitioner considers this sanction to be remedial.

Petitioner also moves the court for Judgment against respondent on account of Petitioner's reasonable attorney fees and actual costs incurred herein supported by petitioner's affidavit as set forth herein below.

DATED this _____ day of _____, 20____.

AFFIDAVIT

STATE OF [STATE NAME]   )

)

[City Name] of [County Name]   )

       I, _____, hereby swear the following to be true: I am the Petitioner herein. Respondent is my _____[former husband/boyfriend/wife/girlfriend]. We were divorced pursuant to a Judgment and Decree of Dissolution of Marriage entered herein on or about [Date], OR, we ended our relationship on or about (Date), and a child support order was issued by the court on or about [Date].

       Paragraph 4 of the court's Judgment reads as follows:

       "4. That the respondent is hereby ordered to pay support to the Petitioner in the amount of $____ per month for the care, support and maintenance of said minor child, payable through the County State Probation Department; Child Support Division in monthly payments of $____ each on the 1st of each month, until each child is emancipated in accordance with State Law, and is no longer attending school on a regular basis. All support payments shall be in the form of cash or check made payable to Support Services, with the first such installment to be paid on or before [Date]."

       Respondent has failed and refused to pay any child support as ordered by the court despite repeated demand that he/she do so.

       Based on the above, I believe respondent is in willful contempt of the decree of dissolution and therefore I ask that he/she be adjudged in contempt of court. In addition, I ask that the court impose all of the following sanctions, all of which I consider to be remedial in nature:

       a. Requiring respondent to pay a sum of money sufficient to compensate me for loss, injuries, or costs suffered by me as a result of respondent's contempt of court.

       b. Confining respondent in the Any County Jail or other appropriate facility for so long as his contempt continues or six months, whichever is shorter.

       c. Requiring respondent to pay an amount not to exceed $500 or 1 percent of his annual gross income, whichever is greater, for each day that he/she remains in contempt of court. I ask the court that this sanction be imposed to compensate me for the effects of his/her continuing contempt.

       d. Any order designed to ensure compliance with a prior order of the court including probation.

       e. Any other additional sanction if the court determines that the sanction would be an effective remedy for the contempt.

       f. Awarding me judgment against respondent for all of my attorney fees, costs, and disbursements incurred in this matter.

_____, Petitioner

SUBSCRIBED AND SWORN to before me this _____ day of _____, 20___.

_____

NOTARY PUBLIC   My Commission Expires: _____

Item #17: Affidavit

ORDER TO SHOW CAUSE, RE: CONTEMPT

IN THE CIRCUIT COURT OF [STATE NAME]
FOR THE COUNTY OF [COUNTY NAME]

STATE OF [STATE NAME]	)	
	)	No.000
[YOUR NAME]	)	
Plaintiff,	)	
	)	ORDER TO APPEAR TO
vs.	)	ANSWER CONTEMPT OF
	)	COURT CHARGE—FAILURE
[OBLIGOR'S NAME]	)	TO OBEY SUPPORT ORDER
Defendant.	)	
	)	

TO:

On the Motion of the Plaintiff,

YOU ARE ORDERED TO APPEAR in person before the Court, [County Courthouse Name, Address, City, State], and show cause why you should not be adjudged guilty of contempt of Court for disobeying the support order entered in the above-entitled Court and cause.

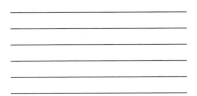
BE PREPARED TO TESTIFY REGARDING
YOUR FINANCIAL POSITION. BRING
WITH YOU ANY RECORDS YOU MAY
HAVE IN CONNECTION WITH YOUR
INCOME, ASSETS, EXPENSES, AND
SUPPORT PAYMENTS.

NOTICE TO DEFENDANT: You are entitled to be represented by an attorney at the Court hearing. If you desire an attorney but cannot afford one, the Court will appoint legal counsel for you.

Dated this _____ day of _____, 20___

_____
Circuit Court Judge

what the government can do for you

there are other methods of collection that can be utilized to get child support that is in arrears. These are methods that are only available to you through a government agency. You must have a current child support order and be using the state child support agencies to collect your child support in order for these government methods to work for you.

tax refund intercept

Federal law allows for the interception of an obligor's federal tax refund if there is overdue child support in the amount of $150 or more. Think of it as a wage garnishment against a tax refund check. If you are receiving your child support through the state child support agency and you are due at least $150 from the obligor, tell your case-worker that you would like to have his tax refund intercepted. The caseworker will check to see if you have a child support order that is still in effect. If you do, you will be asked to sign an affidavit stating the amount of child support that is past due to you. The caseworker will also verify that the agency has the correct address for the obligor. If the address that you have is not current, the current address must be obtained before the intercept can take place.

When the address has been corrected, a letter is then mailed to the obligor advising him that the tax refund will be intercepted for the purpose of collecting past-due child support. Advising the obligor of the intent to intercept allows him an opportunity to contest the action. If the obligor decides to contest the interception, he can only have two defenses that can hold up in court:

1. The obligor can object because he does not owe the amount of child support that is stated. In this case, he would have to prove it by producing receipts of paid child support for the months that you say that it was not paid.

2. He can object because he is not the person that is named on the complaint. In this instance, the case of mistaken identity would have to be proven.

Your obligor may feel that because he currently is making timely child support payments and is slowly paying off past-due support, that a tax refund should not be intercepted. This is not the case, and it is not the law.

Unfortunately, most likely you will only be able to use the inter-ception once as a means of getting past-due child support. Once your obligor is on to you, there is little chance that he will leave money in the hands of the federal government for you to get. Many obligors will at this time decide to change the status on their W-2 forms so as not to overpay taxes during the year. Instead, he would rather owe the government and make payment during tax time. Some may decide not to file their taxes at all.

If the obligor has filed taxes with a new spouse, the intercept will still be made. The spouse will then be able to contact the IRS and have the portion that is rightfully hers refunded. The portion will be determined by the amount of income shown on the income tax forms. (In the meantime, it would be nice to be a fly on the wall when that letter comes through.)

The IRS intercept has accounted for more than 20 percent of all child support collected since 1981. The beauty of it is that it works like a charm, the downside is that it is not an automatically implemented tool—you must personally request that it be done. You must also request it many months in advance. Each state submits a case list to the IRS in August, along with the amount of the arrearages for an interception the following year, so you must plan far in advance. If your state or the state in which your obligor lives requires a state income tax to be filed, then check with your caseworker about intercepting that refund as well.

irs collection procedure

This is a good method of collecting past-due support, but as with every other method, it is not without its downsides. For openers, your case must be handled by the state child support agency, or you must be on, or eligible for, welfare. Your case must be at least $750 in arrearages and it must be at least six months since you last asked for IRS collection assistance. Finally, you must provide identification information on the obligor and the IRS must have reason to believe that the obligor has assets that can be levied.

Once this checklist has been completed, someone from the IRS will attempt to contact the obligor to make a satisfactory arrangement. Sometimes the contact of an IRS agent is all a deadbeat needs to whip into shape. He will suddenly go out of his way to find the money to pay you. After all, now that the IRS is involved, child support seems like a serious issue. If IRS contact doesn't shape him up, the agent will then send a notice of intent to levy any and all nonexempt property that the obligor may have. This is the same as you executing on the obligor's personal and real property, only the IRS is doing it now. Very few obligees use this IRS collection procedure and very few know that it exists. If your child support arrearages are on the high end and the assets that your obligor has are also on the high end, definitely use this method.

The IRS can also be used to locate the obligor and/or his assets. This can be done by doing a search on 1099 matches with names, Social Security Numbers, and wages. Those who are self-employed file 1099 forms with the IRS as opposed to W2 forms, for example. A 1099 is a means of reporting to the IRS your income and assets. If you have income from other sources outside of the wages that you earn (stocks, CDs, money markets, etc.) it would be reported on a 1099 as well. It would also have the addresses that the obligor has reported to the outside source of income. This is useful because he may not report his correct address to the IRS if he knows that you are after him. He may report the correct address to the income sources, however, so as to receive statements and quarterly reports.

Now, let's say that the obligor is less than truthful when reporting to the IRS about additional income sources. Maybe he doesn't list them all, only listing ones that have old address information or that earn little money. The IRS has another procedure called the 1098. The 1098 reports to the IRS the interest that taxpayers pay on any certain account. So even if the obligor doesn't report it, the IRS has a way of finding it, and through that they may uncover a correct address or an asset gold mine.

There are downsides to both the 1099 and the 1098 information and asset location. You can only request that these searches be done if previous information has been requested of the IRS, but the obligor has still not been located. Also, the information can be used for location purposes only, and cannot be used to execute on found assets of the obligor. The way to get around this, however, is to subpoena the financial institution where the assets are located. The financial institution must at that time give you whatever information you request, even if it is information that you already have but can't legally use.

chapter 12

afdc & child support

Seventy-five percent of women on AFDC (Aid to Families with Dependent Children, also known as welfare) receive public services because the absent parent of their children is unable or refuses to pay child support. In order to qualify for AFDC, normally you must own less than a total of $1,000 in non-exempt property and have few resources and limited income. If you have any income at all while you are receiving public benefits, it is deducted from your monthly allowance to ensure that you pay the state back for any money that they give to you during your time of need. Consider it a signature loan. Just sign on the dotted line and you get the help that you need, but at some point in the future it must be paid back. If you own a home and are given an AFDC grant, the state will attach a lien on your property for the amount that you have been given. When you sell your house, you will have to pay back the money that you received while on welfare.

the $50 disregard

The only exception to this rule is the "$50 disregard." The first $50 of any payment that you receive, per month, from any income source is disregarded as income. Child support is considered income, as is any money that anyone gives to you as a gift. If you are able to get a part-time job earning $75 per month, you will be allowed to keep the first $50 of that amount while the balance must be given to the state. Likewise, if you are able to get any child support from the obligor while you are on public assistance, you will get to keep the first $50. Whether the obligor makes the payment in full or only a partial payment for the month is irrelevant, you get the first $50 either way.

in-kind payments

If anyone makes payments on your behalf, say for your car, rent, or cable bill, they are not considered to be income unless the money touches your hands. If you are lucky enough to have someone who is willing to subsidize a better apartment for you or a safe vehicle to drive, have that person make the payments directly. Payments made to your accounts by someone else on your behalf are called in-kind payments.

assignment of rights

If you are on AFDC, you have assigned the rights of your child support case to the state. This is true whether you came to the state with a child support order already in place or if they are helping you to establish an order. The state now has control of your case. You are no longer the beneficiary of your child support, the state is. State employees are the ones who will now decide what happens with it or, more likely, what doesn't happen with it. They have the right to decide what collection will be used to get money from your obligor and whether they want to go after him at all. They can do this without consulting you. If they are receiving any child support at all, whether it is the full amount or not, whether they can get more or not, they may decide that they don't wish to pursue the case anymore and settle for the small amount of money that they get.

To be fair, it should be noted that the state agencies have more cases than they can effectively handle. It stands to reason that everyone doesn't get the best care this way. But that doesn't do your case any good and there is absolutely nothing that you can do about it. You can jump up and down, scream and shout, and tell your caseworker of the $400 per week raise that the obligor just got. If he doesn't want to pursue it, he doesn't have to. He owns your case. You can't get a modification, wage garnishment, or take your obligor to court unless the caseworker agrees to it. What's even worse, you may not be able to get the slightest bit of information on your case either.

When you apply for AFDC benefits you won't be told that you are signing your rights away, although you are. If you had an attorney to represent you as you were signing up for benefits, he would have been able to tell you exactly what you were signing. But, of course, that's not the case since you needed every penny that you had at the time. I hate to be the bearer of bad news, but it's important that you know this before you try to start any kind of legal proceedings.

If you find yourself in this position, you can do one of two things:

1. Do nothing and accept your AFDC benefits. If you are on welfare, you must need the assistance. You probably can't afford to refuse benefits and pursue child support on your own.

2. If you strongly believe that you can handle your case better than the state has and you are willing to take the gamble of relinquishing your AFDC payments to pursue your child support—which could take months in some cases—then go for it. Many have succeeded this way.

The bottom line is this: you can't go after your obligor on your own if you are on welfare. Only you can decide if it will be worth your while to do without the benefits while you are chasing your deadbeat for money. If you are able to get child support from your obligor, will it be enough to sustain you? Will you be able to get it regularly or will you have to employ several collection methods to squeeze the money out of him? Find your answers, then make your best decision.

chapter 13

interstate child support collection

It is much easier to collect child support if the obligor lives in the same state as you do. If you know where he lives and works, a wage withholding is an easy method of collecting your support payments. If you do not know where the obligor lives or works, or if you need to do some sleuthing to find either the obligor or his assets, it's more difficult if he lives far away from you. However, there are some commonly known and widely used collections techniques you can employ if the obligor does not live in the same state as you.

interstate wage withholding

The interstate wage withholding is the most popular method of collection. It works the same way that a wage withholding works if the obligor lives in the same state that you do. The only difference is that you must cross state lines in order to collect the money. The *originating state* (the state in which you live, also called the *initiating state*) does not have *jurisdiction* over someone who does not live there, so it cannot withhold his wages. Instead, your state must petition (ask) the obligor's state to withhold wages for child support and forward them to the state where you live. If the state child support collection agency is collecting your support for you, they will receive the payment and then forward it to you. If you are handling your own case, the payment will go directly to you.

The drawback with this method is that most states do not respond immediately when petitioned for help on a child support case. Often these procedures take months and can prove to be frustrating. The originating state is kept in the dark about whatever collection methods are, or are not, being used by the *responding state*. Generally, the originating state will send a transmittal by mail to the responding state once action has been taken on some collection method. But this is not guaranteed and even a small correspondence of this nature can take months on behalf of the originating state. Your caseworker and your state are left to wonder and so are you. Even though your caseworker cannot take direct action on your child support case if it is out of state, the interstate wage withholding is still the most effective method to use. Your decision at this point would be whether you want to handle your case yourself, so that all of the correspondence must go to you, or whether you want the state agency to handle your case for you.

If you want to file for an interstate wage withholding yourself and you already have a child support order and an order for a wage withholding, you must provide the following documentation:

1. Certified copy of the original child support order

2. Certified copy of the order for a wage withholding

3. An affidavit from you testifying to the amount of arrearage and the supporting documentation that goes along with it, or a certified copy of the payment record from the state agency that was collecting your support payments

4. The full name and current address of the obligor

5. The name and address of the obligor's employer

6. The name and address of the obligee (you)

This information must be provided to the responding state in order to file a *foreign order* of support. A foreign order of support, simply stated, is a support order that you have obtained that you would like to enforce in another state. A child support order that you received in your state is not good in any other state unless you have it registered in the state where you will try to enforce it. If the obligor moves from state to state, you will have to register your child support order in each state before you attempt to collect on it. Think of it as a vehicle registration. Your car may be properly registered in your own state, but if you move to another state, you must have it registered there before you can consider it legally registered. Unfortunately, this is how our child support system works right now. The procedure to get a wage withholding on the income of an obligor who lives out of state is as follows:

1. Send the above documents to the withholding agency in the state where the obligor works. (Although most states will accept this documentation from you, there are some states that will only accept it from a government agency.)

2. The support order will then be entered by the responding state.

3. You must then send notice to the obligor that you are intending to withhold his wages. If you need to refresh you memory on how to do this, see Chapter 9.

4. As long as the obligor does not contest the wage withholding, an order will be sent to the obligor's employer.

These procedures can seem very complicated to most people. If you have any questions or are unsure about what do to at any time, you will probably be better off letting the state child support collection agency help you.

uniform enforcement of foreign judgment act

A final judgment is a judgment for a sum that cannot change—it is final. Ongoing child support payments are not final, they continue until the child reaches the age of majority. If you take an obligor to court for past-due child support and win your case, a judgment will be entered for the amount of child support that is past due. That amount cannot change. If the obligor continues to add arrearages, the amount that he owes you will continue to change, but the judgment amount will not. It is final. If you want to increase the judgment amount then you will have to return to court. If you have a final judgment for child support arrearages that you would like to collect under the Uniform Enforcement of Foreign Judgment Act, you can bring an action to enforce a foreign judgment in another state. Just as you must register a wage withholding in the new state before you can collect on it, you must register your judgment as well. The Uniform Enforcement of Foreign Judgment Act can only be used for final judgments. Following are the steps you must take to pursue an enforcement of foreign judgment.

1. Call the clerk of the court where the obligor lives and ask whether a copy of a certified judgment will be accepted, or whether it must be authenticated. Authenticated means that the clerk and judge of the originating state certify the document to be an authentic copy. According to the responding clerk's standards, obtain a copy of the judgment (see Item #19) and mail it.

2. File a statement giving the name and current address of the obligor.

3. The clerk will then notify the obligor that you have filed a foreign judgment and will supply a copy of the judgment.

4. The obligor will then have up to twenty days (depending on the state) to contest the judgment. If he does not, you can then proceed with collection techniques.

uniform reciprocal enforcement of support act

The *Uniform Reciprocal Enforcement of Support Act*, or URESA, is a law that allows you to file for current child support, back support, a modification of your child support award, medical expenses, and custody/visitation, without leaving your own state. It is the same as applying for services through your local child support agency, asking them to collect support due from someone who lives in the same state as you do. The difference is that URESA only handles *interstate cases*. When you petition through URESA, they will file your documentation with the obligor's state and have someone represent you at the hearing where the absent parent/obligor resides.

You can apply for services from URESA through your state child support collection agency. At that time you will be assigned a caseworker who will be the main source of communication between yourself and the responding state.

You can also apply yourself, or through an attorney, by calling the family court in your area and asking where you must go in your area to apply for services.

long arm statutes

Many people do not know about *long arm statutes*, though if they did, they could eliminate a lot of the heartache that goes along with collecting across state lines. If your obligor lives out of state, you must have your judgment(s) registered in the state where the obligor lives before you can attempt to collect any money. Let's say that not only does your obligor live out of state but also has a vacation house in the same state in which you live. If that were the case, you would not have to have the judgment(s) registered in the other state, because the obligor has a legal residence in the state where the judgment was written. If the obligor lived in another state, but worked in your state, the same would apply. Now let's say that the obligor lives 2,500 miles away and works in the same state in which he lives. The company that he works for is a large company with branches in over twenty-five states, and one of those branches is in the state where you live. Since your state has jurisdiction over the company that is doing business in your state, it can order the company to do many things, and one of those things is to pay your child support. In a case like this you could save yourself the time of registering your judgment somewhere else in order to get your support money.

Long arm statutes can vary from state to state. Though they may not be universally accepted, it can't hurt you to try. The most you can get out of it is to collect your child support, the least it can get you is nothing, which is what you have right now.

NOTICE OF FILING OF FOREIGN JUDGMENT

IN THE CIRCUIT COURT OF THE STATE OF [STATE NAME]
FOR THE COUNTY OF [COUNTY NAME]

In the matter of:	)	
[YOUR NAME],	)	No. 000
Petitioner,	)	NOTICE OF FILING OF
	)	FOREIGN JUDGMENT
and	)	
[OBLIGOR'S NAME],	)	
Respondent	)	

COMES NOW the petitioner and gives notice to respondent of the filing of the judgment rendered in the Circuit Court of the State of [State Name] on [Date], a copy of which is attached hereto.

DATED this _____ day of _____, 20____.

_____
[Your Name], Petitioner

AFFIDAVIT

STATE OF [STATE NAME]	)
	)
County of [County Name]	)

[Your Name], Petitioner, makes this affidavit under oath.

On [Date], a judgment was rendered by the Circuit Court of [State Name] styled "In re the Marriage of [Your Last Name] in favor of [Your Name] against [Obligor's Name] in the amount of $____"

The name and last known address of the Judgment Debtor is as follows:

[Obligor's Name
Address
City, State   Zip Code]

[Your Name
Address
City, State   Zip Code]

SIGNED this ___ day of _____, 20_____

_____
[Your Name], Petitioner

Item #19: Notice of Filing of Foreign Judgment   163

collecting from the self-employed

If your obligor is self-employed, you have a unique set of issues and problems when it comes to child support enforcement. The self-employed obligor cannot have his wages withheld, because, under the law, technically he does not earn "wages." When you take him to court for child support, you may not be able to get a fair amount of support in proportion to his earnings because he may legally not report all business earnings. Unless you do some research, you may not even know that the obligor is running a business at all.

When it comes to self-employed obligors who don't want to pay, you have to pull out the heavy artillery. Strict enforcement techniques that have been outlined in Chapters 9, 10, and 11, will have to be used to collect from the unyielding self-employed obligor.

Assuming that you have utilized all methods that you could (or are in the process of doing so presently), the following are some methods that you can use to take money directly from the obligor's business.

Keep in mind that you cannot put the obligor out of business. The obligor's business is exempt $12,000 from the various collection methods that you may use against him. So, if the obligor only has $12,000 in business assets (or less) you cannot take anything from the business. If he has more than $12,000, then you can put your plans into action.

For example, if the obligor has $10,000 in business property and $2,500 in cash in an account for a total of $12,500, you will only be able to get $500 from the business. But, of course, that's $500 more than you had before and $500 less that he owes you. Furthermore, in the event you seize and/or garnish more than you will be allowed to keep (if you take $12,500 in the above example but you can only keep $500), you will succeed in making the obligor's life difficult for a few days while the courts free the money you have tied up. Personally, I like the idea. Aren't you being inconvenienced by having to chase the obligor for the money in the first place? And, if you are asked why you seized more money than you could keep, say what my daughter says when she makes an honest error…whoopsie!

Onward and upward! The following methods are great ones to use against those who run their own businesses. Just keep in mind that this does not include those who run corporations, which are protected from the personal offenses of the obligor.

bank accounts

If the obligor is operating a sole proprietorship, he is using his own Social Security Number for business tax records. Since that is the case, anything that the business owns, the obligor owns as well. You can garnish business accounts containing available cash.

business property

You can also seize and sell business property. For example, if the obligor is running a local mechanics shop that has equipment worth a lot of money, re-read Chapter 9 and go to work on a seize-and-sell. Company equipment is not the only sort of item that can fall prey to being seized and sold. Any kind of office equipment, inventory, and furniture can be seized for the payment of child support.

till-tap

If the obligor is running a business with a cash register, have the sheriff conduct a till-tap. Remember to wait until the busiest season and the busiest time of day to reap the most benefit from this.

business suppliers

If you are fortunate enough to know who some of the obligor's suppliers are, you are ahead of the game. If you don't, do some research to find out. Then subpoena them for whatever information you can. If you find that the obligor is paying for shipments of goods, you can place a lien on whatever shipment(s) that the obligor has paid for. Of course, the obligor will be as mad as a lunatic, but after all, that's what you want. He will have no other choice but to pay you so that you release the lien, or watch his business go down the tubes. (You will, of course, attach a lien on every shipment with every supplier that he has until you are paid in full.) If the shoe is on the other foot and your obligor is the supplier, you can garnish the payment that the obligor is due to receive from the company he is supplying.

The previous collection methods listed are methods that used *leverage* over the obligor. If you have leverage, the obligor may be willing to give you what you want just to get you off of his back. Some examples of leverage may be:

• If you are certain that the obligor is not reporting a portion of his income, you can threaten to gather proof and call the IRS.

• If the obligor is an immigrant and his visa has expired, you can threaten to call immigration.

You know the obligor better than I do. Find his soft spot and then go for the jugular. Don't hold back and don't feel badly that you have caused so much misery for him. He isn't exactly feeling sorry for you and your children when you eat soup for supper every night. If that were the case, you would already have the child support that you need.

collecting from the unemployed and underemployed

There are many obligees who complain that they cannot get any child support from their obligor because he doesn't have a job. There are others who complain that they cannot get enough child support or that the arrearages will never go away, because the obligor does not make enough money. They say that they cannot get blood from a stone. I say that they have not learned the best way to squeeze. In more instances than not, though it may be a long wait at times, you can get child support—even from an unemployed obligor. The following items outline some of the many ways you can cash in on "other incomes" to get child support from someone who is unemployed or underemployed.

- **Unemployment** In most states, a portion of an obligor's unemployment benefits can be withheld for child support.
- **Disability** If the obligor is receiving disability benefits, you and/or your child may be entitled to benefits as well. Contact your local Social Security office for an appointment to find out.
- **Veterans' Benefits** Contact the regional office closest to you. In most instances, veteran's benefits cannot be held for child support. There are some complicated exceptions to this rule, so before you decide not to bother, contact them and let them figure it out for you. If you have an attorney involved, of course, seek his assistance as well.
- **Life Insurance Policies** If the obligor has a life insurance policy that can eventually be cashed in, that policy can be garnished for past-due support and withheld for future support payments depending on the amount of the policy.
- **Assets** If the obligor has assets that are worth you going through the trouble of seizing and selling (especially real estate), move to have a lien placed on the property and foreclose if it comes to it.
- **Inheritance** This may seem morbid, but if you can't get any money from the obligor, you may get some from his parents or someone else who may leave him money in a will. If you continually update your judgment in court so that the proper amount is reflected at the time you can collect the money, you will be able to receive interest from day one to the day you get your child support. Be sure to ask the judge for pre-judgment interest as well as post-judgment interest.
- **Lottery Winnings** You don't have to be in it to win it. New Jersey and California have begun to garnish the lottery winnings of those who owe child support.

Of course, these are only some of the ways that you can get blood from your own stone. If you think about it for awhile, considering what you know about the obligor, I'm sure that you can think of some yourself.

collecting from the military

If you are trying to collect child support from someone who is in the military, there is good news and there is bad news. The good news is that the military has policies toward family support and the policies are good ones. Each branch of the military, which includes the Army, Navy, Air Force, Marines, and Coast Guard, insists that its personnel support their families back home. The bad news is that it can be difficult to locate a military employee at times and when you do, superior officers are not always as helpful as they should be.

If you know where the obligor is stationed, half of your battle is over. Write a letter to the soldier's commanding officer. Let him know that you have a judgment for a child support order. Supply your name, address, a copy of the judgment, the soldier's name, and his service number. Request that the commanding officer assist you in obtaining your support.

In some instances, the commanding officer will help you by having the appropriate amount of child support withheld from the soldier's pay (without a wage withholding order) and forwarded to you. In other instances, you will be sent away and told to obtain a wage withholding prior to being helped. Unfortunately, you cannot send a wage withholding to the military yourself—it will not be accepted. You must use the services of the child support agencies. Once the wage withholding is received at the proper branch, you can expect to get payments after sixty days.

If you do not want to use the child support agencies and are not getting any help from the soldier's commanding officer, there are other people to contact who may help. If you are in a bind and need immediate financial assistance, contact the Red Cross and/or the Army Relief Fund. These organizations have emergency funds available to assist the families of military employees. You will need to provide your child support order, your name and address, and the soldier's name, address, and service number, if you have it. Also contact the inspector general. The inspector general is someone who can put pressure on the obligor's commanding officer for not doing his job properly, and can get your money on the way to you quickly.

If you do not have a judgment for a child support order and you are married (and the law can assume paternity) but separated from your spouse, you may be able to get child support anyway. Ask the commanding officer when you write to him.

If you do not know where the obligor is stationed, you can find out by contacting the recruitment office where the obligor enlisted. This information is a matter of public record. If you know where the obligor has been assigned, call the "installation locator" at that particular installation. Then call the number that you are given and ask for the soldier's unit of assignment.

If you still have not been able to locate the soldier, try the military locator services listed in the back of this book.

collecting internationally

Collecting child support is difficult if you have to cross state lines. Imagine the difficulty you will have if you have to cross borders or oceans to other countries to collect your support payments. The United States is not the only country that has to deal with issues of child support or child support enforcement. Luckily for you, other countries have this problem as well. Because of this, and because their citizens sometimes cross the border into the United States seeking refuge from having to pay child support, they are, at times, willing to set up agreements to enforce foreign child support orders.

There are no formal agreements between the U.S. and other countries for the payment of child support, although there are some countries that the U.S. has reciprocity with, and others with whom the U.S. is developing such a relationship. Many of the fifty states have been utilizing URESA for the collection of child support in other countries. Under URESA, a child support judgment from the United States is treated as a foreign judgment in another country. Once it is registered, the responding jurisdiction (in this case, the foreign country) will reciprocate by using URESA practices to sue the obligor for child support or enforce the existing order. As you learned in Chapter 13, if this action were to take place between two states it would be considered the enforcement of a Foreign Judgment Act. Between two countries it is *comity*. Comity is the practice of a country recognizing the law of another country within its own jurisdiction.

This is not to say that all countries will allow comity. There are a few countries that will allow the enforcement of a foreign child support order, but there are also many that will not. The rule of thumb is that if the country has the same or a "substantially similar law" in effect, they will probably allow comity.

Arrangements have been made with the following countries:
Canada
France
United Kingdom
Norway
Sweden
Hungary
Poland

The following countries have arrangements in process:
Israel
Italy

Austria
Spain
Portugal
Belgium
Denmark
Czechoslovakia
Yugoslavia
The Netherlands

I'm sorry to say that if your obligor has fled the country, you have a long road ahead of you when it comes to child support collection. If you have the money, the best thing that you can do in this situation is to hire an attorney in the country where the obligor has fled (remember the home court advantage). If you are able, also hire an attorney in your state to represent you here. If you do not have the means to hire an attorney or two, use the services of the child support enforcement agencies.

collecting from a federal employee

Collecting child support from a civilian federal employee can be one of the worst things you can attempt to do. The government makes it difficult, if not impossible, for anyone to attempt to get money involuntarily from one of its own. They will return court documents unanswered if information they want was not included. When they do allow a garnishment, they will only allow it to be taken from the employee's net (take-home) pay, which includes other deductions like retirement, life insurance, savings plans, etc., rather than the employee's gross pay. Once all deductions have been made, there may not be anything left to garnish. When serving a federal employee, if the documents are not sent to the proper office and to the proper person, they will be returned. At the same time, the government has laws that state that federal employees cannot be overdue in payments on a debt. The best thing that you can do when you are dealing with the federal government, or one of its employees, is to use the government laws to your advantage when you can and beat them at their own game.

• Prior to serving a wage withholding, visit your local library and ask the reference librarian to help you find Code Federal Regulation 5 CFR Part 581. It has the address for every executive federal branch. Locate the branch that your obligor works in. You will be able to use the address you have found to properly serve him.

• Mail the wage withholding return receipt certified mail from the post office. Expect to pay a small fee of about $3 for this service. Along with your wage withholding, include the obligor's name, date of birth, Social Security Number, civil service retirement number (if there is one), veteran's claim number (if there is one), and advise the office where he works. Also include your name, address, a copy of the judgment, and the purpose of the judgment.

• If you want to circumvent the system, contact the civilian employee's supervisor by mail and request her assistance collecting your support. Gently remind her that Code Federal Regulation 5 CFR Part 2635.809 prohibits the indebtedness of federal employees and subjects them to discipline for failure to pay their debts. Also remind her that Code Federal Regulations 5 CFR Part 735.203 prohibits conduct by a federal employee that may be prejudicial to the government. This may get you some action from the supervisor. Of course, in order for an employee to be disciplined for failing to pay his debts, it must somehow interfere with the employee's job performance. And, of course, it will, if the employee has to go to court several times for the non-payment of child support.

If the obligor is not a federal employee, but does business with the federal government by way of contract, you are out of luck. Government contractors are exempted from garnishments of any kind. Other methods of child support collection outlined in Chapters 10 through 13 will have to be utilized.

If your deadbeat is a federal employee and you are having a difficult time locating him, there is a special Internet locator that you can use: www.fic.info.gov. If you don't have access to the Internet, try calling (800)688-9889. This number is simply an information line for various government services, but if you happen to get someone nice on the phone (and you are very sweet) they may be inclined to help you out.

when an obligor files for bankruptcy

When I was working in collections for the bank, the people I was collecting from often told me that they were in bankruptcy. If a person files for bankruptcy, all collection attempts must stop immediately. This is called an *automatic stay*. If they continue, it can be construed as harassment and there can be penalties. This is true when it comes to child support collection as well. If the obligor files for bankruptcy, you can no longer pursue child support collection until you go to court to apply for a "relief" from the "stay."

A person, or a company, can file for bankruptcy to either have all debts *discharged* (eliminated), or to have a "stay" from the collection procedures until the debts can be slowly paid off over time. Child support cannot ever be discharged, but it can be paid off at a slower pace. If your obligor has filed for bankruptcy, it will be handled in one of the following ways:

Chapter 7: Chapter 7 is the bankruptcy type where all of the debts are discharged. The obligor starts off with a clean slate with no debts. Child support is an *undischargeable* debt. Seek immediate relief from the bankruptcy court by using the Motion for Relief from Stay (Item #20).

Chapter 11: Chapter 11 is mostly for businesses that are in over their heads. They can propose a reorganization to the bankruptcy judge where they outline how their debts will be paid off. If the judge approves it, they then go into a Chapter 11. If the judge does not accept their proposal, then the bankruptcy becomes a Chapter 7.

Chapter 13: Chapter 13 is similar to the Chapter 11, but it is for individuals. It works the same way in that the individual filing for a bankruptcy must outline how all outstanding debts will be paid. If accepted, the individual can keep his personal property, if not, it is liquidated.

In all three instances you are entitled to a relief from the stay. If the obligor has filed for a Chapter 13, all past child support owed will be reorganized under the plan. You cannot continue to attempt collection on that amount. Current child support and future child support cannot be reorganized, so those full amounts are still due to you. For example, if the obligor filed for bankruptcy on the first of the month owing you $3,000 with $500 due the first of every month, he would still owe you $500 when the next month rolls around. The past due $3,000 would be reorganized with the bankruptcy judge and you would have to accept whatever payment arrangement the judge puts in place.

Filing a relief from a stay costs about $70 and must be done at the clerk's office. Remember to serve a copy to the obligor, his attorney, if there is one, and the trustee. The notice that you receive informing you of the obligor's upcoming bankruptcy proceeding will provide you with the names and addresses of the people whom you need to serve. Remember, bankruptcy is a federal action and is filed in federal court, unlike your petitions regarding child support, which are filed in state court.

MOTION FOR RELIEF FROM STAY

[Your Name
Your Street Address
City, State, Zip Code
Your Telephone]

IN THE UNITED STATES BANKRUPTCY COURT
FOR THE [DISTRICT NUMBER] DISTRICT

In Re	)	
	)	Case No.
[OBLIGOR'S NAME],	)	
	)	
	)	Contested Proceeding
	)	No.
Debtor.	)	
	)	
[YOUR NAME],	)	MOTION FOR
	)	RELIEF FROM STAY
Plaintiff	)	
v.	)	
	)	
[OBLIGOR'S NAME],	)	
	)	
Defendant	)	

TO: The Honorable _____ Bankruptcy Judge:
COMES NOW Plaintiff [Your Name] and moves the Court for an Order for relief from the automatic stay order so that child support may be collected in State Court proceedings from the earnings and assets of the Debtor which are not property of the estate.

PLAINTIFF [YOUR NAME] alleges, moves, and requests:

1.

That on [Date], the above-entitled Debtor, filed a voluntary Petition in Bankruptcy in above-entitled Court and was adjudged a Bankrupt on or about the same date.

2.

The Bankruptcy Court has jurisdiction over this proceeding pursuant to 11 USC 362.

3.

That the Debtor's Chapter 13 was confirmed by the Court.

4.

The Plaintiff was listed as a creditor in the schedules of liabilities filed therein by said Bankrupt and was in fact as unsecured creditor of said Bankrupt at the date of the filing of said voluntary Petition in Bankruptcy in the amount of $_____.

5.

That the nature of said unsecured debt owing by Bankrupt to plaintiff is child support arising out of an order issued [Date], by the Circuit Court of the State of [State Name] in and for the City of [City Name, County

Name]. By the terms of said judgment and order for child support the Bankrupt was to pay $_____ per month for the support of the minor child(ren) commencing [Date].

6.

That Plaintiff, a Judgment Creditor of the Bankrupt debtor, received a judgment on [Date], as set forth in paragraph 5 herein above plus interest thereon.

7.

That the aforesaid Judgment and order is a judgment and order determining defendant Bankrupt debtor's obligation for present child support and past accrued reimbursement of child support and as such is non-dischargeable by virtue of 11 USC 523(a)(5)(A) as amended, 42 USC 656(b) as amended, and 42 USC 602(a)(26).

8.

That between [Date] and the date Bankrupt filed his voluntary Petition in Bankruptcy, the Bankrupt paid a total of $_____ on account of his said on-going above-mentioned child support obligation and $_____ on account of said child support reimbursement arrearage obligation.

That between the date when the Bankrupt filed his voluntary Petition in Bankruptcy and the date of this motion, the Bankrupt has paid a total of $_____ on account of his said on-going above-mentioned child support obligation and $_____ on account of said child support reimbursement arrearage obligation.

10.

There was due and owing on the date of filing of the voluntary Petition in Bankruptcy by the Bankrupt the sum of $_____ principal plus interest thereon from [Date], in child support reimbursement arrearages.

11.

That the Chapter 13 plan of the Debtor makes no provision for child support and for $_____ monthly to be applied to the arrears as a general unsecured claim.

12.

The Bankrupt has sufficient income to make the scheduled monthly payment of $_____ to the Trustee of the arrearage and also pay said ongoing child support. Due to the automatic stay, plaintiff is unable to enforce the herein above-mentioned order for child support against the earnings and property of the Bankrupt which are not property of the estate.

It is therefore respectfully requested that plaintiff's motion be granted and the stay order previously imposed be partially vacated insofar as it operates to prevent enforcement by plaintiff of the hereinabove referenced order for child support in the State court against earnings and other property of the debtor that are not property of the estate.

DATED this _____ day of _____, 20____.

_____

[Your Name]

effective complaining

When all else fails and the child support enforcement agency is not doing its job to its fullest potential, you can always complain. Complaining in an inefficient manner, or to the wrong people, will not get you anywhere. Complaining effectively will. This chapter is about learning how to effectively complain, and how to complain to people who can help you.

Before considering a complaint to anyone, be sure that you have accurate records to support your positions, and be attentive in your record keeping. Here is a list to help you keep impeccable records.

• Keep a log of every conversation that you have with a case-worker or anyone else with whom you may speak at the agency. The log should state what was said during the conversation, what action the caseworker promised, and when he told you to follow up (after you asked). It should also have the date and time that the conversation took place. Case log example:

2/20/98 9:30A.M. Spoke with Martin, he said that he does not have any new information. I told him that I was able to locate Dan's new home address and work address. He said that he will get to work on a wage withholding. As he suggested, I will follow up with him in 2 weeks.

3/7/98 9:45A.M. Martin says that he hasn't had time to do a wage withholding because he has so many cases to work on. He told me to follow up with him in 2 weeks.

3/21/98 3:25P.M. Martin was not at his desk, so I left a message.

3/21/98 4:00P.M. Martin was not at his desk, so I left a message.

3/22/98 9:05A.M. Martin said that he would check into the matter, but he didn't get back to me as he promised. I faxed a letter to him and his supervisor.

3/23/98 10:40A.M. Glenda, Martin's supervisor, returned my call to say that a wage withholding has been put into effect.

The case log has shown many things. It gives an account of what transpired between client and caseworker. This way, you won't have to rely on your memory to put details together, and you will also be better informed. By having the accurate dates of when you spoke with your caseworker the last time, you won't let too much time go by without a necessary phone call. The time of day that you normally reach your caseworker gives you an indication of when he is likely to be reachable.

• Keep copies of anything and everything that you must forward to your caseworker, whether it is information on the obligor or a complaint letter that you sent to the caseworker or supervisor.

• When sending a complaint letter to your caseworker or the caseworker's supervisor, speed up the process by sending it by fax if you have one available to you. A faxed document will get to your caseworker immediately, rather than waiting for "snail mail" through the post office. If you don't have a fax machine accessible to you, use the regular mail service.

• If you must send a complaint letter to someone higher than your caseworker's supervisor, send it by fax, but also send it return receipt certified mail from the post office. You will get a notice in the mail of when your letter was received at the child support agency and they will know that you mean business.

• Every letter that you send to your caseworker should be carbon copied to the caseworker's supervisor. At the bottom of the letter that you are sending, underneath your signature, type "cc: [supervisor's name]" and then send a duplicate of the letter to the supervisor. This accomplishes two things: first, it lets the caseworker know that you are keeping his supervisor informed; and second, it advises the supervisor of all proceedings with the case. In the event that you will have to complain, the supervisor should not be surprised and should be well-equipped to handle it.

• When you do get the action on your case that was promised, be sure to write a quick thank you note to whomever it was that brought about the action.

The chain of command should go like this:

1. First complain to the caseworker (Item #21). If you are able to speak with him, ask when would be a good time to follow up. Do not

get off the phone without asking for a follow-up date no matter what he says. Do not let him blow you off. Unless he is waiting for action from a responding state, a follow-up date generally should be no more than two weeks later. If the caseworker does not respond to you at all, wait two weeks before you take the next step.

2. If the caseworker does not do as promised, or if you are otherwise unhappy with the results that you have gotten, complain to the caseworker's supervisor (Item #22). If the caseworker's supervisor does not prove helpful, wait two weeks before taking the next step up the rung.

3. The caseworker's supervisor's manager is the next person that you would contact (Item #23). Telephone contact is usually the first method of contact, followed by any letters that you will send. If you end up sending a letter to the caseworker's supervisor's manager, be sure to also "cc:" both the caseworker and the caseworker's supervisor, so that they can expect to hear from the big boss. In my experience, many cases do not go beyond this point. If yours does, the Appendix section in the back of this book will have the proper chain of command. In addition to contacting the proper officials who can get action on your case within the child support enforcement offices, also contact your elected officials (Item #24). Elected officials can put pressure on the child support enforcement office to get the job done. Begin with your congressperson and/or senator.

Not only must you know the proper people to whom to speak/write, you must also know the best way to write a complaint letter so that it gets the attention it deserves. Many obligees write long letters about how her ex left home, kicked the dog, smacked the kids, and took off in the car. Sorry to say, but the caseworker isn't interested in your sob story. There are about a hundred that come across his desk every day and half of them are probably worse than yours. The only information that your caseworker is interested in is the facts. Be short and sweet, but firm.

Date

[Caseworker's Name
Name Of Child Support Agency
Street Address
City, State, Zip]
Re: Case Number [Your Case Number]

Dear [Caseworker's Name]:

      I spoke with you last week on [Date], and you promised me that you would have a wage withholding done on my case. We agreed that I should follow up today. When I called your office you told me that you had not had a chance to do the wage withholding because you have so many cases. Since you promised to do this last week and did not do so, please be certain to do it now. I have been waiting far too long for my child support. If you need to reach me, please call me at home, [Your Phone Number]. Thank you for your time.

      Sincerely,

      [Your Name]

cc: [Supervisor's Name], Supervisor

Item #21: Sample Complaint Letter to Caseworker

[Date]

[Name of Caseworker's Supervisor
Name of Child Support Agency
Street Address
City, State, Zip]
Re: Case Number [Your Case Number]

Dear [Caseworker's Supervisor's name],

      I am writing to you for help with my case. On [Date], I spoke with my caseworker [caseworker's name] and he promised that he would initialize a wage withholding against my ex-husband for child support. It is now a month later and a wage withholding has not been done and I have not been able to get [caseworker's name] on the phone.

      I understand that [caseworker's name] has many cases to work on but he did promise to get this done for me on that day. Can you please look into this matter for me and have the withholding done immediately? If there is a problem that prevents this from happening or if you need to speak with me for any reason, please do not hesitate to contact me. I can be reached at home at [Your phone number]. Thank you for your time.

      Sincerely,

      [Your name]

cc: [Caseworker's name]

[Date]

[Caseworker's Supervisor's Manager's Name
Name of Child Support Agency
Street Address
City, State, Zip]
Re: Case Number [Your Case Number]

Dear [Caseworker's Supervisor's Manager's Name]:

I have become very frustrated with the progress on my case and with your agency. I am not receiving any action on my case, and I do not get a response from my caseworker or my caseworker's supervisor when I call or when I write.

At this time, I am requesting a copy of my case log so that I can see what activity has taken place on my case. I am also asking that a wage withholding be done on the obligor's income. I provided my caseworker with this information a month ago. Thank you for your time.

Sincerely,

[Your Name]

cc: [Caseworker's Name], Caseworker
        [Supervisor's Name], Supervisor

deadbeats

[Date]

[Government Official's Name
Street Address
City, State, Zip]

Dear [Government Official's Name]:

  Enclosed you will find correspondence between the Child Support Enforcement Agency and myself. As you will see, I have not had much action on my case and I have provided everything that I can to the agency. It has been 120 days since I have asked them to run a state and a federal locator to find a current address for my former husband. Although the law provides for 75 days to conduct a search, they still have not gotten back to me. Telephone calls and letters to their office remain unanswered.

  Please help me with my case.

  Sincerely,

  [Your Name]

cc: [Caseworker's Supervisor's Manager
County Child Support Office
Street Address
City, State, Zip]

glossary

Abnormal specimen testing A method of paternity testing that can be done on a deceased body to determine DNA matching for paternity.

Absent parent A parent who does not live with his/her children, but has financial responsibility for them. Also known as the non-custodial parent.

AFDC/ADC (Aid to Families with Dependent Children) Financial assistance (welfare) for families that have children who are deprived of the financial support of one of their parents by reason of death, disability, or continued absence.

Affidavit A written declaration, or statement of fact, made under oath, or in the presence of an officer authorized to make declarations under oath.

Appeal A request that a case be transferred to a higher court, for another hearing.

Arrearages Unpaid child support payments owed by a parent who has been ordered to pay.

Automatic stay The process by which a legal proceeding in progress must immediately come to an end.

Buccal swab sampling A method of DNA matching, for the purpose of determining paternity, in which a large cotton swab is brushed along the inside of the cheek, collecting skin cells that can be tested for matching DNA.

Change in circumstances A change in the financial circumstances of either the non-custodial or the custodial parent, deeming the present child support order unfair.

Child support award An amount of money that a non-custodial parent has been ordered by a court of law to pay for the upkeep of his/her children.

Child support enforcement agency A state-run government agency that collects child support payments for custodial parents.

Comity The practice by which one state or country recognizes the judgments or decisions of another, although they do not have to legally. It is a show of good faith.

Consent agreement Voluntary written admission of paternity, or responsibility for child support.

Court-ordered Terminology used when the court has made a decision and handed down a ruling.

Creditor's bill A legal motion that must be filed with the court to prove that a person or entity is in possession of property that belongs to another person or entity.

Credit reporting agency An agency that reports one person's timely and late indebtedness to others, for the purpose of establishing credit-worthiness.

Custodial parent Parent with whom the child lives, and who has legal custody of the child.

Custody Legal determination that establishes with whom a child should live.

Default Failure of a defendant to file an answer, response, or appeal in a civil case within a certain number of days, after having been served with a summons and complaint. Results in an automatic judgment in favor of the plaintiff.

Default judgment Decision made by the court when the defendant fails to respond.

Defendant The person against whom a civil or criminal proceeding is begun.

Deposition A question and answer period that is conducted under oath.

Discharged The terminology used in bankruptcy when a debt is eliminated.

DNA matching A method of familial relationship determination in which genetic chromosomal material is matched for its hereditary pattern.

Downward modification The terminology for a previously awarded child support amount being lowered.

Enforcement Forcing payment of a child support or medical support obligation.

Establish paternity The process of having paternity proved and established in a court of law.

Estoppel A law that says that once a decision has been made in a court of law, you cannot go back and ask that it be changed based on information that you had when the decision was made.

Execution Enforcement of a civil money judgment by ordering a sheriff to seize and sell the debtor's real or personal property.

Family calculation A method of DNA matching for the purpose of paternity testing in which immediate family members of the suspected father are matched along with the child in question. This is normally done when the suspected father is not available for DNA matching.

Federal Parent Locator Service (FPLS) A service provided by the federal government through the Office of Child Support Enforcement (OCSE) for the purpose of searching Federal Government records to locate absent parents.

Foreign order A judgment determined in a state or country other than your own.

Forensic paternity testing Methods of DNA matching for the purpose of paternity that can be done in the absence of the suspected father.

Garnishee The person, or entity, in possession of property that belongs to a debtor and upon whom a garnishment is served.

Garnishment A legal proceeding whereby a portion of a person's wages, or other assets, is withheld and applied to payment of a debt.

Guidelines Standard methods for setting child support obligations based on the income of the parent(s) and other factors as determined by state law.

Hearing An appearance before a judge, hearing officer, or administrative other.

Indigent A condition of being poor or needy. Also a person who is poor or needy.

Initiating state The state in which a proceeding is commenced and where the custodial parent is located.

Interstate case A child support case in which the custodial parent and the non-custodial parent live in two different states.

Interstate wage withholding A child support case in which a wage withholding is sent from one state to another to be processed.

Judgment A legal decision made by the court. Also known as an order.

Jurisdiction Legal authority that a court has over particular persons, certain types of cases, and in a defined geographical area.

Legal father A man who is recognized by law as the male parent.

Legislation The making of laws.

Letter of consent Voluntary written admission of paternity or responsibility for support.

Leverage The use of power or effectiveness to enhance one's capacity.

Lien A claim upon property to prevent sale or transfer until a debt is satisfied.

Long arm statute A law that permits one state to claim personal jurisdiction over someone who lives in another state.

Medical support A legal provision for payment of medical and dental bills—can be linked to a parent's access to medical insurance.

Modify To change.

Motion An application to a judge for an order or a hearing.

Non-AFDC case A case where an application for child support enforcement has been filed and the family is not receiving public assistance.

Non-custodial parent The parent who does not have primary custody of a child, but who has a responsibility for financial support.

Obligation Amount of money ordered by the court to be paid by the responsible parent and the manner in which it is to be paid.

Obligee A custodial parent or guardian who has been awarded a child support order by the court.

Obligor A non-custodial parent who has been ordered by the court to pay child support.

Offset An amount of money taken from a parent's state or federal income tax refund to satisfy a child support debt.

Order A judgment handed down from a judge or other officer of the court.

Originating state The state from which legal documents originate.

Paternity Male parentage.

Paternity judgment Legal determination of fatherhood.

Paternity test A test that can determine male parentage.

Plaintiff A person who brings an action, complains, or sues in a civil case.

Pro se The act of representing yourself during a court proceeding.

Public assistance Money granted to individuals or families for living expenses, based on need.

Responding state A state receiving and acting on an interstate child support case.

Retainer A fee paid to retain an attorney's services.

Serve (service of process) The delivery of a summons or other notice to a person or entity.

Show cause A court order directing a person to appear and bring evidence to offer reasons why a court order should not be executed. A show cause order is usually based upon a motion and affidavit asking for relief.

State Parent Locator Service (SPLS) A service operated by the state to locate absent parents.

Subpoena An official document ordering a person to appear in court or to bring and/or send documents.

Summons A notice to a defendant that an action against him/her has commenced.

Title IV-D Title IV-D of the Social Security Act is the portion covering the child support enforcement program.

Title IV-D agency A state agency that collects child support for custodial parents under Title IV-D.

Transcript A typewritten copy of a deposition.

Undischargeable A debt that cannot be discharged under the bankruptcy law.

Unearned income Income that a person or entity receives that has not been earned by way of employment.

Uniform Reciprocal Enforcement of Support Act (URESA) A law which allows a custodial parent who lives in one state to establish and enforce a child support order against a non-custodial parent who lives in another state.

Upward modification The terminology for a previously awarded child support amount being increased.

Visitation The right of a non-custodial parent to visit or spend time with his/her children.

Volunteer agreements An agreement made between a custodial parent and a non-custodial parent for the payment of child support; made in lieu of a formal child support order.

Wage withholding Procedure by which automatic deductions are made from wages or income to pay a debt such as child support; may be voluntary or involuntary.

Writ An order issuing from a court and requiring the performance of a specific act, or giving authority and permission to have it done.

Written interrogatory A deposition that is conducted through the mail.

state child support enforcement offices

As of September 1999

ALABAMA
Bureau of Child Support
Dept. of Human Services
50 Ripley
Montgomery, AL 36130
(800) 284-4347

ALASKA
Child Support Enforcement Div.
Dept. of Revenue
550 West 7th Ave., 4th Fl.
Anchorage, AK
(907) 269-6900

ARIZONA
Child Support Enforcement Administration
Dept. of Economic Security
P.O. Box 6123/Site Code 776-A
2222 W. Encanto
Phoenix, AZ 85005
(602) 252-4045

ARKANSAS
Officer of Child Support Enforcement
Arkansas Social Services
P.O. Box 8133
Little Rock, AR 72203
(800) 264-2445
(501) 682-8398

CALIFORNIA
Division of Child Support
Department of Social Services
744 P Street/Mail Stop 9-011
Sacramento, CA 95814
(916) 657-3661

COLORADO
Department of Human Services
Division of Child Support
303 E. 17th Ave; Suite 200
Denver, CO 80203-1241
(720) 947-5000

CONNECTICUT
Bureau of Child Support Enforcement
Dept. of Human Resources
999 Asylum Avenue
Hartford, CT 06105
(800) 228-5437

DELAWARE
Division of Child Support
Dept. of Health & Social Services
P.O. Box 904
New Castle, DE 19720
(800) 464-4357 (In State)
(800) 273-9500 (Out of State)
(302) 577-4800

DISTRICT OF COLUMBIA
Office of Corporation Counsel
Child Support Enforcement Division
441 4th Street N.W. 5th Floor
Washington, D.C. 20001
(202) 724-1444

FLORIDA
Office of Child Support Enforcement
2410 Allen Road
Tallahassee, Fl 32399-0700
(800) 622-5437

GEORGIA
Office of Child Support Enforcement
878 Peach Street N.E.
Atlanta, GA 30309
(800) 227-7993
(404) 654-2780

GUAM
Office of the Attorney General
Union Bank
194 Hernan Cortez Avenue
Agana, Guam 96910
(671) 477-2036

HAWAII
Child Support Enforcement Agency
Department of Attorney General
601 Kamokia Blvd; Suite 251
Kapolei, HI 96805
(888) 317-9081
(808) 586-1500

IDAHO
Bureau of Child Support Enforcement
Department of Health & Welfare
450 W. State Street, 6th Floor
Pete T. Cenarrusa Building
Boise, ID 83702
(800) 356-9868
(208) 334-5710

ILLINOIS
Bureau of Child Support Enforcement
Illinois Department of Public Aid
509 S. 6th Street
Springfield, Illinois 62701
(800) 447-4278
(217) 524-4602

INDIANA
Child Support Enforcement Division
Department of Public Welfare
402 N. Washington Street
Room W360
Indianapolis, IN 46204
(800) 840-8757
(317) 232-4885

IOWA
Bureau of Collections
Iowa Department of Human Services
727 E. 2nd Street
Des Moines, IA 50309
(888) 229-9223
(515) 242-5530

KANSAS
Child Support Enforcement Program
Dept. of Social & Rehabilitation Services
P.O. Box 497
Topeka, KS 66601-0497
(785) 296-3237

KENTUCKY
Division of Child Support Enforcement
P.O. Box 2150
Frankfort, KY 40602
(800) 248-1163
(502) 564-2285

LOUISIANA
Support Enforcement Services
Department of Social Services
P.O. Box 829
Baton Rouge, LA 70821
(225) 342-5760

MAINE
Support Enforcement and Location
Bureau of Social Welfare
Department of Human Services
State House, Station 11
Augusta, ME 04333
(800) 371-3101
(207) 287-2886

MARYLAND
Child Support Enforcement Administration
Department of Human Resources
311 W. Saratoga, 3rd Floor
Baltimore, MD 21201
(800) 234-1528
(410) 767-7674

MASSACHUSETTS
Child Support Enforcement Unit
Department of Revenue/CSE
P.O. Box 4068
Wakefield, MA 01880
(800) 332-2733

MICHIGAN
Office of Child Support
Department of Social Services
235 S. Grand Avenue
P.O. Box 30478
Lansing, MI 48909
(517) 373-7570

MINNESOTA
Office of Child Support
Department of Human Services
444 Lafayette, 4th Floor
St. Paul, MN 55155
(651) 296-2542

MISSISSIPPI
Child Support Division
State Department of Public Works
939 N. President
Jackson, MS 39202
(601) 965-1200

MISSOURI
Child Support Enforcement Unit
P.O. Box 1527
Jefferson City, MO 65102
(573) 751-4301

MONTANA
Child Support Enforcement Program
P.O. Box 5955
Helena, MT 59604
(800) 346-5437
(406) 444-4614

NEBRASKA
Child Support Enforcement Office
P.O. Box 95026
Lincoln, NE 68509
(402) 471-9125

NEVADA
Child Support Enforcement Program
District Attorney's Office
885 E. Musser St., Suite 2030A
Carson City, NV 89710
(775) 887-2099
(775) 887-2098

NEW HAMPSHIRE
Office of Child Support Enforcement Services
129 Pleasant St.
Concord, NH 03301
(800) 852-3345 ext. 14427

NEW JERSEY
New Jersey Division of Public Welfare
Bureau of Child Support & Paternity
P.O. Box 716
Trenton, NJ 08625
(609) 588-2385

NEW MEXICO
Child Support Enforcement Bureau
Department of Human Services
P.O. Box 25109
Santa Fe, NM 87504
(800) 288-7207
(505) 827-7200

NEW YORK
Office of Child Support Enforcement
40 W. Pearl St., 13th Floor
Albany, NY 12260
(800) 343-8859
(518) 474-9081

NORTH CAROLINA
Child Support Enforcement Section
Division of Social Services
100 E. Six Forks
Raleigh, NC 27609
(919) 571-4120

NORTH DAKOTA
Child Support Enforcement Agency
Regional Child Support
State Capital
P.O. Box 5518
Bismark, ND 58506
(701) 222-6721

OHIO
Bureau of Child Support
373 S. High Street
13th Floor
Columbus, OH 43215
(614) 462-3275
(800) 827-3740

OKLAHOMA
Division of Child Support
Department of Human Services
P.O. Box 53552
Oklahoma City, OK 73152
(405) 522-5871

OREGON
Recovery Services Section
Adult and Family Services
1495 Edgewater Street NW
Suite 290
Salem, OR 97304
(503) 378-4489

PENNSYLVANIA
Child Support Programs
Dept. of Public Welfare
1303 N. 7th St.
P.O. Box 8018
Harrisburg, PA 17105-8018
(717) 783-8729
(800) 932-0211

PUERTO RICO
Child Support Enforcement Program
CALL Box 3349
San Juan, PR 00904
(809) 722-4731

RHODE ISLAND
Bureau of Family Support
77 Dorance
Providence, RI 02903
(401) 222-2409

SOUTH CAROLINA
Child Support Enforcement Division
P.O. Box 1469
Columbia, SC 29202-1469
(803) 898-9336
(800) 768-5858

SOUTH DAKOTA
Office of Child Support Enforcement
700 Governors Drive, Suite 84
Pierre, SD 57501-2291
(605) 773-3641

TENNESSEE
Child Support Services
Citizens Plaza Bldg., 12th Floor
400 Deadrick Street
Nashville, TN 37248-7400
(615) 313-4880
(800) 838-6911

TEXAS
Child Support Enforcement
c/o Attorney General's Office
P.O. Box 12017
Austin, TX 78711-2017
(512) 231-4600
(800) 252-8014

UTAH
Office of Recovery Services
120 N. 200 West
P.O. Box 45011
Salt Lake City, UT 84145
(801) 538-4400

VERMONT
Child Support Division
Department of Social Welfare
103 South Main Street
Waterbury, VT 05671-1901
(802) 241-2319
(800) 786-3214

VIRGIN ISLANDS
Support and Paternity Division
Department of Justice
48B-50C Kronprindsens Gade
GERS Complex–2nd Floor
St. Thomas, VI 00802
(809) 776-0372

VIRGINIA
Division of Support Services
8007 Discovery Drive
Richmond, VA 23288
(800) 468-8894

WASHINGTON
Office of Support Enforcement
P.O. Box 9162
Olympia, WA 98507-9162
(360) 664-5000
(800) 457-6202

WEST VIRGINIA
Office of Child Support Enforcement
State Capital Complex
Building #6, Room 812
Charleston, WV 25305
(304) 348-3780

WISCONSIN
Division of Community Services
Office of Child Support
201 E. Washington Avenue, Rm. 271
Madison, WI 53707-7935
(608) 266-9909

WYOMING
Child Support Enforcement Section
Hathaway Bldg.
Cheyenne, WY 82002
(307) 777-7892

appendix c:

military locator service

United States Army
USA Enlisted Records & Evaluation Center
8899 E. 56th Street
Indianapolis, IN 46249-5301
(706) 325-3732

United States Air Force
AFPC-MSIMDL
550 C Street
Randolf Air Force Base, TX 78150-4752
(210) 565-2660

Navy Personnel Command
Pers 312
5720 Integrity Blvd.
Millington, TN 38055-3120
(901) 874-3388

United States Marine Corps
Headquarters USMC MMSB10
2008 Elliot Road. Suite 201
Quantico, VA 22134-5030
(703) 784-3942

United States Coast Guard
2100 Second Street S.W.
Washington, D.C. 20593
(202) 267-2229

frequently asked questions

Does child support have to be paid through the enforcement agency, or can my ex pay me directly?

Your ex can pay you directly if that is an arrangement that you both can live with. Before you make that decision, consider that if payments are made by wage withholding, you will have a clear payment record through the CSE office, payments won't be delayed by the mail, and you avoid the possibility of money falling into the arrears by an ex who does not pay because wage withholdings are automatic. As long as the obligor keeps his job, you will receive child support. Having a wage withholding is beneficial for the payor as well, due to some incidents of the payee not reporting the actual amount of support received.

Do I need a lawyer to petition for child support?

Having an attorney is not a prerequisite when petitioning for child support. If you can afford to hire one—which may be costly—then it is always recommended that you do so. However, you may always represent yourself in court, or use one of many creative ways of hiring an attorney which may cost you nothing at all, or the bare minimum in up-front fees. See Chapters 5 and 6.

What is the difference between alimony and child support?
Alimony is a sum of money paid each month to a former spouse for her direct benefit. It could be used in a rehabilitative sense so that the receiver can go back to school to further enhance a career or change careers, or it can be used to keep the receiver up to the standard of living to which she has been accustomed. Child support is an amount of money paid to the custodial parent for the care of the children born to the payor and the payee.

Does it cost anything to apply for Child Support Enforcement services?
Anyone who is receiving AFDC, Medicaid, or Foster Care stipends does not have to pay for CSE services. Everyone else can be charged a fee of up to $25. Some states absorb all, or part, of the fee, and some states will collect the fee from the non-custodial parent. Check with your local CSE agency regarding your state policy.

Does it cost anything to receive services from CSE agencies?
CSE agencies can recover all, or part, of their fees from those who do not receive AFDC benefits. Fees can be deducted from child support payments, or collected from the non-custodial parent. Not all states recover the costs of their services so it's important to check with your local agencies regarding your state policies.

Do I need to know any of this since I have a lawyer?
Absolutely. You are always your own best advocate. By being well-informed and knowledgeable about child support guidelines and law, you can be certain that you ask the right questions and act on what is in your best interest.

If my child support is in arrears, can I withhold visitation?

No. Child support and visitation are separate issues. You cannot lawfully withhold visitation if child support is past due. Conversely, one cannot lawfully withhold child support if not allowed visitation. Many states are working on methods to assist with visitation issues.

What are the benefits of establishing paternity?

Once paternity has been established, your child gains most of the legal rights that a child born within a marriage has. This includes, but is not limited to, child support, rights to the father's medical and life insurance benefits, inheritance, Social Security, and veterans' benefits. For more on paternity, see Chapter 2.

What if the alleged father denies paternity and refuses to take a paternity test?

As of October 1989, anyone involved in a contested paternity case must submit to genetic testing. If the accused father is served and fails to respond to the complaint against him, a default judgment will be entered in court establishing paternity. At the same time, a court order for support may be issued.

Can I have an attorney and still receive CSE services?

Yes. Your attorney can work with the CSE agency on your behalf.

Will I receive child support collected if I am on AFDC?

If you are on AFDC and the state is able to collect your child support, you will receive up to $50 each month from the support collected in addition to your regular grant from AFDC. The balance of the child support paid will go towards reimbursing the government for the benefits paid to your family.

My ex owes me a lot of child support, but continuously shows up with brand new cars. How could this be allowed to happen? Aren't creditors aware of child support arrearages?

Not unless someone tells them! A report of child support arrearages must be made to the credit bureaus or they will not be properly informed. The law allows for child support arrearages to be placed on credit reports so creditors can be aware of their customers' complete financial picture. Someone just has to make it happen. See Chapter 9 to learn how to do this.

My ex pays me directly, but the child support checks always bounce. By the time I get paid it is always another thirty days or so. What can I do?

The law allows for a wage withholding when child support payments are thirty days or more behind. Child support payments would then be taken directly from your ex's pay, eliminating the need for him to pay you directly. Also, it is a crime to bounce checks. Think about taking criminal action by reporting the bad check to your local police department.

What if my ex's employer refuses to withhold wages for child support?

Your ex's employer does not have a choice. Federal law dictates that an employer must withhold wages if ordered by a court to do so.

My ex owed me several thousand dollars before I took my case to the CSE agency. Is there any way to recoup that past-due money?
Since the money was owed before the CSE agency became involved in your case, it will have to verify that the money is owed to you. What documentation do you have to prove your case? Bring whatever letter of agreements that you have pertaining to this matter to your caseworker. You may have to appear in court to present your documentation before any collection can take place.

My ex is incarcerated. Is there any way for me to receive child support payments?
Child support obligations are not discontinued if the obligor is unable to make the payments. The unpaid support will accrue until it is properly paid, unless you agree to have payments deferred until the non-custodial parent is released and working. But why would you do that? If while in prison there are wages earned through a work release program, these earnings can be garnished for child support. If the non-custodial parent has assets or real property, you can receive an execution whereby the property is seized and sold, and whatever support is owed to you is then paid. This can be complicated, and cost you some money. Only you can decide if it is worth it. See Chapter 9.

My ex threatened to file for bankruptcy if I continued to pursue child support. How would this affect me?
It may affect you and it may not. If it does affect you, there are different degrees to which it can and will. See Chapter 19.

My CSE agency is not doing all that it can do to enforce my case. Can I take it to federal court?

Yes. If your CSE agency has not had any response to requests for enforcement in another jurisdiction, you can take your case to federal court. The decision has to be made by the Federal Regional Office of Child Support Enforcement at the request of your caseworker and the State Enforcement Office. If you are not satisfied with the services you are receiving at your local CSE agency, ask your state agency for help. For more on effective complaining to CSE agencies, see Chapter 20.

index

about the author

Simone Spence is a nationally recognized leader in the field of child support enforcement. The impact from her groundbreaking research has given her a national presence. She is sought after as a speaker and lecturer, and is a frequent guest on radio and television programs. Ms. Spence writes, consults, and is the founder of the Spence Foundation, a national agency for the enforcement of child support. She lives in the greater New York area with her husband and children.

If you would like to be placed on the waiting list for a personal consultation with Ms. Spence, please contact her at 973-509-6975.

Also, be sure to visit www.spencefoundation.org, where you will find "EZ kits" with pre-printed forms ready to be filed with the court. There are forms for child support, divorce, paternity testing (as well as "at-home" testing kits), credit repair, and bankruptcy. You will also find a full range of deadbeat greeting cards and the "Deadbeat Hall of Shame." Visit for products or just for fun!

If you have comments or want to be on the Spence Foundation mailing list for upcoming events and seminars, send your request to:

Spence Foundation
Box 5
Cedar Grove, NJ 07009

Ms. Spence offers seminars, training, and workshops free of charge to government officials, mental health professionals, and social service agencies on a limited basis. Please contact her in writing on official letterhead for more information.